The Bush Still Burns

THE BUSH STILL BURNS

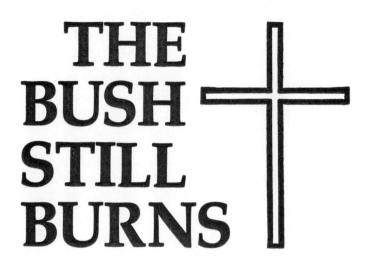

How God Speaks to Us Today

JOHN F. SMITH

SHEED ANDREWS AND McMEEL, INC.
Subsidiary of Universal Press Syndicate
KANSAS CITY

Library of Congress Cataloging in Publication Data
Smith, John Ferris.
  The bush still burns.

   1. Spiritual life—Anglican authors. 2. Prayer.
I. Title.
BV4501.2.S5342   248′. 48′3   77-18007
ISBN 0-8362-0761-0

For

MARY GRACE
SARAH AND PRISCILLA

CONTENTS

ACKNOWLEDGMENTS

I owe a debt of thanks to many people who helped with this book, but principally to the Danforth Foundation for an Underwood grant and the Diocese of Massachusetts for a Continuing Education grant, both of which enabled me to take the time for reading and writing. I am also grateful to James Carroll, a colleague in nearly everything, for his encouragement, enthusiasm, and ideas, and to Frank Burke, SJ, for a great deal of counsel and advice. I cannot let this opportunity go by without a special word of appreciation to the people who are Boston University, who are the community out of which this was written. And acknowledgment is made to the following sources for permission to quote their material:

"Chorus" from *For the Time Being*, p. 308, W.H. Auden, *Collected Poems*, copyright © 1976 by Edward Mendelson, William Meredith and Monroe K. Spears, executors of the Estate of W.H. Auden, published by Random House, Inc., New York
Lines from "September 1, 1939," p. 58, *The Collected Poetry of W.H. Auden*, copyright © 1945 by W.H. Auden, Random House, Inc., New York

 **PREFACE**

Moses was looking after the flock of Jethro, his father-in-law. He led his flock to the far side of the wilderness and came to Horeb, the mountain of God. There the angel of Yahweh appeared to him in the shape of a flame of fire, coming from the middle of a bush. Moses looked; there was the bush blazing but it was not being burnt up. "I must go and look at this strange sight," Moses said, "and see why the bush is not burnt." Now Yahweh saw him go forward to look, and God called to him from the middle of the bush. "Moses, Moses!" he said. "Here I am," he answered. "Come no nearer," he said. "Take off your shoes, for the place on which you stand is holy ground. I am the God of your father," he said, "the God of Abraham, the God of Isaac and the God of Jacob." (Exodus 3:1-5)

In the first few chapters of Exodus, we read the familiar story of Moses, of his birth while his people were enslaved by Pharaoh, how he was hidden in the bulrushes to escape the murderous edict against boy children, how he was found and adopted by Pharaoh's daughter, how growing up he raised his arm to protect the defenseless, how he was exiled and settled down to minding his father-in-law's cattle. And finally we read how it was that one day he led his cattle "to the far side of the wilderness," and there saw a bush burning and heard a voice calling his name.

Biblical critics have pointed out that there is a red bush in that region which grows vaguely in the shape of a flame. Those of us who wait for the Word from God know that the critics have missed the point of the story and the miracle. A miracle is not that a bush will burn without being destroyed. Miracles are changes in the nature of men and women; their possibility lies in human hearts which are open to being addressed by God. That coincidence of God's reaching out and man's hearing was Moses' miracle and is the miracle of our humanity in Jesus Christ.

We have come to a time when many persons feel that their hearts are the site of ashes, that the bush has indeed been destroyed; the fire of love and hope has burned out. Those places in us in which once the "sweet birds sang" are now "bare ruined choirs" and the visions we had now appear to be "love in ruins."

It is no coincidence that novels of disillusion and despair or of barely attained personal survival are among the books that many individuals respond to strongly, for the point of view they express is realistic. Death, wielding his terrible sword of despair, is powerful in the world in which we live. Death's burned-out victims are all around us, young and old. They are not only the poor and the powerless—many persons who enjoy great advantages feel that life has come to hold little promise for them, that there is little hope for the future. Where I work, in a university community, those feelings are rife. Faculty and others who once were full of life now are obsessed with the notion that they must build a career, not live out a vocation. They say, "It's no fun any more."

For many Americans, life is no fun anymore. It is no fun to be rich in a poor world, oppressors in an oppressed world, not if you are thoughtful and morally sensitive. It is no fun being a man when maleness is, however correctly or incorrectly, under attack. That word, "fun," which on one level refers only to a kind of childish frivolity, comes to convey also the notion that life is somehow worth living, that it is worth making a run at. The "fun" of the challenge of making a life, of trying to make things better, reaches into the depths of who we are, and today we are having a difficult time finding that kind of fun. Meanwhile, commercial efforts to provide distraction and entertainment, such as television and Disney World, become more and more strained and grotesque. The Citizens Band radio fad, which on one level provides a delightful distraction from the dreariness of long-distance driving and an opportunity for people to reach out and help one another, on another level tends to become a substitute for true identity ("What's your handle?") and real community. In short, sooner or later, everything leaves a sour taste in our mouth. "How all occasions do inform against me, and spur my dull revenge," says Hamlet, speaking of a moment in his life when, "The best lack all conviction, while the worst are full of passionate intensity." So it is with many of us. We only have to remember how we felt as we watched recent political conventions.

But the purpose of this book is to insist that the bush still burns; that the vision still has power to raise up those who are dead in mind and conscience. "Sure, he that made us with such large discourse, looking before and after, gave us not that capability and godlike reason to (grow musty) in us unused," says Hamlet. The People of God still look to Him to call us by our name and give us the gift he gave Moses, His own Name, the Word of Life itself.

The bush still burns.

INTRODUCTION
"If you only knew . . ."

He is the Way
Follow Him through the Land of Unlikeness;
You will see rare beasts, and have unique
adventures.

W. H. Auden, *For the Time Being*

I f you only knew . . ." After I grade the first paper my freshman students hand to me, I try to soften the blow a little and get to know them by asking them about themselves. Seeing your precious creative effort torn to pieces quite cheerfully and thoughtfully before your eyes can be a trying experience for anyone and I think it important to be reassuring and interested at such a time. But every conversation comes to the same point, no matter if the grade is high or low. The student always shakes his head and says, "If you only knew . . . ." What each thought I had better know, because I would find out sooner or later, is that he was a fake and phony.

I was usually only trying to ask them, nicely, if they had expected the grades they got. But they heard another, more important, question, and to my amazement each came as to a confessional to say, if the paper was good, that he wasn't really a good student, that he didn't study hard, probably couldn't write, was good only at manipulating his teachers to get good grades. If the paper was bad, or maybe just mediocre, he would warn me against expecting anything better from him. Even though these students had convinced the admissions officers they should be admitted into a rather good college, down deep they were not worthy, were not smart in any way. They implied that through various kinds of cunning they had covered up their inadequacies until then, but I had finally got their number. The students with better grades insisted that I would soon find them out and become aware of their inabilities. They were saying, "If you only knew what I'm *really* like."

After I became aware of this reaction to my interest, I decided to put a similar question to clergy and teachers of religion who came to the retreats I conducted. "What do you think about your life? Do you think you live up to the image of ministry to which you aspire?" Over and over again, they answered that they too were fakes and phonies. Now most of them, like the students, were actually living rather exemplary lives. Like the students, they had a high regard for the nature of the enterprise in which they were involved. Most of them wanted to do well, to serve people, and they were good at their jobs. They were not primarily interested in or motivated by social or cultural success or monetary rewards or other false values. They wanted to be—and were, in most cases—good priests or ministers, just as the students were, in fact, good at living out *that* vocation. Both groups understood that being clergy or students was not just a matter of conducting services or reading books, but was also a calling to do things, be active. They took care of people who were in trouble, struggled for peace and justice, worked for better conditions of life in their communities. In short, they tended to act out in their lives that which they professed to believe in as individuals. They tried to be authentically there for others. And they all cared, cared until it hurt, cared to learn, cared to be with others. You could see it in their eyes. By any standard both groups were successful at what they were doing, but both groups thought of themselves as fakes. *If you only knew, each one said.*

The students lacked confidence which one might expect in the young, especially if they are sensitive and if they haven't been admitted to the seven or eight schools in the country to which admission means undoubted success and prestige. But the young persons' perception of themselves was that they weren't competent, couldn't understand the material, probably never would be able to write on the level I expected, were just capable, or not capable of getting acceptable grades. They harbored that terrible accusation of themselves secretly and dreaded the day when the truth would be revealed. "If you only knew . . . ."

The clergymen's secret was that, while they seemed to be good at the outward aspects of their job (counseling, organizing, serving people), they were not holy men and women, not men and women of prayer, and they thought, above all, this is what they ought to be. They felt as though they were fakes and their Christianity was only skin deep. They believed all the stupid and harsh things that had been said about them, especially those who had been active in the civil rights or peace movements. The accusation that they were not authentic clergy because they were interested "in the world" or "politics" was, they suspected, true. They feared that they were, in fact, "only social workers," "cause followers." They half believed that there was no divine imperative to their work, that it was just "politics." And the sticking point, the point that seemed to confirm those terrible suspicions, "If you only knew . . . ," was that they didn't pray. That was the source of their guilt.

The truth is that the clergymen hadn't been able to adapt the medieval models of devotional life they had been taught in seminary to the busy modern world in which they lived because the models were not adaptable. There was neither the right kind of time nor the space to pray like that, even if the content of prayer as they had learned it had been relevant to the issues in which they were involved. The guilt-based medieval models could not meet the needs of a modern world which was searching for a way to relieve oppressive feelings of guilt, for a new identity for humanity, for a change in human nature. As they were unable to pour the old wine into the new wineskins, they blamed themselves. The ministers could not develop the kind of relationship with God they thought they were supposed to have because they were going about it the wrong way, so they gave up on prayer, and thought of themselves as fakes.

Both of these groups had accepted an inaccurate evaluation of themselves from the outside. But it was never an accurate evaluation of their actuality or their potential. The students, given some thought and encouragement—and, most important, some expectation of change on the part of the teacher—usually turned out to be pretty good students. They found they could read perceptively, write reasonably clearly, and talk intelligently about the assigned material. They could find the passion, commitment, and joy which ought to be typical of young people at the height of their physical and mental powers. But they had been taught somewhere to be cynical about their possibilities and about themselves. And that cynicism about the possibilities of living good, creative, and fruitful lives had eroded their self-confidence and left them bored and nervous and despairing.

The clergymen and women had accepted the notion that everyone must have the same sort of religious experience or relationship to God in order to be a servant of God, that everyone must spend a certain amount of time each day at a certain sort of prayer, that we all must constantly speak familiarly of God and of religious experience, that we must all be preoccupied with religious concerns if we are to be faithful people. The patterns and methods of the contemplative life are not for everyone, but our spiritual mentors not only acted as if they were, they failed to develop patterns and methods of prayer and meditation for those in the active life. In turn, many of us were left high and dry on a spiritual desert island and thought of ourselves as frauds and religious failures even though by every sign mentioned in the Scriptures, we have been doing the will of God in healing, reconciling broken relationships, struggling against evil forces, freeing those held in bondage, and proclaiming Good News and hope to the poor.

The only thing that kept us from being more active was the nagging feeling that we ought to be praying more, ought to be more "contemplative," ought to participate in some elaborate spiritual discipline as defined by one of the great mystics, ought to be keeping a "prayer list."

I say that I was fascinated by the misunderstanding that had such power over these marvelous men and women, clergy and students. When I tried to talk to them about themselves, they would simply say, "If you only knew . . . ." They were implying that if I could spend time with them I would discover that they were hollow and I would not like them, respect them, think well of them as, they were sure, God did not.

That "If you only knew . . ." intrigued me. I would respond, "But I do know, I have known."

I had been a student like that, believing that there would be a terrible day of reckoning when my teachers discovered that I was merely clever, merely swift, not profound. On that day I would be found out. I worried about it, carried with me such unspoken anxiety that I never did as well as I should have, and the school year, culminating in exams, was always one long agony of guilt and impending judgment, with the inevitable B+ as the result. I can still remember the exhilaration of the first year when I no longer had to take final exams. But despite it all I knew I loved to read and to study and to know. My number is, and always was, legion.

Years later, when I was asked to teach at Boston University, and worked in the library doing research and delivered a series of lectures which were received with interest and approval, I recapitulated the experience of writing papers and taking exams, only now, because I wasn't trying to live up to some impossible vision or worrying about pleasing a faculty member for a grade, it was fun, even delightful. I realized that much of what had passed for academic profundity was merely pretension and defensiveness. I knew then that I had been taken in by a system which kept out many thoughtful and sensitive people by erecting false barriers. This feeling was confirmed when perfectly intelligent students came in to say to me, "If you only knew . . . ."

I had also been one of those theological students who had tried to pray, had faithfully gone to chapel and retreats and Quiet Days. But the meditations and the talks were always about something that seemed to have nothing to do with what I was doing or with where I was going or, for that matter, with the people I was living and working with. The talks were always all about God, his Peace, his Glory, his Perfection, his Holiness. They were also about how we had to take "even" a few minutes a day for the Lord, had to withdraw into a "quiet place," and be alone with him. Unless we did this, we couldn't possibly be his servants—it was the most important thing anyone could do.

And while I believed and trusted and experienced the presence of God in the people around me and in the company of those with whom I worked—there was always for me a sense of the abiding power of the Spirit in the civil rights movement and in many parts of the peace movement, and in the history of the changes in culture through the sixties—I could never think of myself as one who prayed, as a *real* priest, one who had a relationship with God like the one I had been taught was essential.

In company with hundreds of clergy, I bought devotional books, read the first chapter and stuck them in the bookcase. (The same experience is reported by J. A. T. Robinson in *Honest to God*, and is supposed to have brought him the largest set of common responses to that book.) I adopted devotional disciplines (reading the Daily Office was popular when I was in seminary) then put them aside because I was too busy in erratic ways to be more than perfunctory. I remember that our dachshund chewed up a certain book I was using and somehow I never got around to buying another one. I stopped praying in that way because there were important things to do—not busy work, but important things that had to do with ministering to individuals. It is not too much to say that I was often driven away from "prayer" by the grace of God which sent me into the lives of suffering beings around me. Devotional exercises of the sort I have described were totally irrelevant to the issues that touched my life. By that I mean that they did not bleed when they were cut, and men and women were bleeding all around me.

I am not suggesting that the life of prayer and meditation should be changed so that it "fits in" to our idea of what it ought to be. Karl Barth once said that to speak of man in a loud voice is not to speak of God. But I *am* suggesting that the presence of God is in the events of history and in the events of our personal lives—in *events* as much as in a relationship. It is in those events that we sense the presence of the risen Lord. We know his resurrection when we know his presence in the events of our own history. I want to suggest a way of looking at prayer that assumes his presence and looks for ways of knowing him and being known. Therefore, I am not so concerned with our knowledge of God as I am with the realization of his knowledge of us.

I conclude that the students and clergy of whom I speak were both laboring under false expectations and accepting false evaluations. In each case, it was necessary to suggest that they were listening to the wrong voices. Because those voices spoke with the intonation of senior faculty or upper administration or bishops or "spiritual directors" or gurus did not mean that they were right, or even faithful to the revelation of God. Those voices said things like, "you have to let go and let God . . ." or "All this peace and civil rights stuff, what's this got to do with the *real thing*?" or "Students just don't know enough to criticize the President," or "The college chaplains are good on social action, but what about important things, like vandalism in the dormitory?"

The students and the clergy assumed that the self-defined spiritual gurus of our time are correct instead of trusting themselves, the scriptural record, or the Spirit. They allow others to define them instead of taking responsibility before God for their own lives.

My experience with the students and clergy led me to decide that it was necessary to come at the life of prayer and meditation from a new angle. (Actually, it's not new, it just hasn't been the conventional wisdom.) One would begin with the experiences and events of life as the basic material for prayer and meditation.

"If you only knew. . . ." I decided to take as a beginning point what I "only knew."

The story of how I came to pray, to be able finally to say the word "prayer" without feeling like a phony is not really long or very complicated, and it is told later on in this book as it developed out of thinking and praying and learning.

For that is what this book is about: how a person might come to praying out of the raw material of his or her life, finding those roots and that sense of being known which grounds him or her in the presence of God and sends him out into the presence of God and holds her together in unity by the presence of God.

These lines from W. H. Auden are an entrance song:

He is the Way
Follow Him through the land of Unlikeness
You will see rare beasts and have unique adventures.

And, singing, I invite you to the adventure.

CHAPTER ONE

The Kingdom of Anxiety

He is the truth
Seek Him in the Kingdom of Anxiety
You will come to a great city that has expected
your return for many years.

W. H. Auden, *For the Time Being*

I said that we would start with the truth: our feelings of guilt and phoniness at being Christians who have a hard time praying in the ways we were taught it was proper and correct to pray, and who have therefore given up praying. We were told that if we were to be Christians who (insisted on) living in the world, we must develop a kind of alternation of quiet times and busy times. This is, I suspect, so that we would not be too caught up in the concerns of the world and lose sight of "heaven." We were to set aside quiet times to be with God and busy times to be with people, and the goal was to carry the quiet times (God) into the busy times (people). Sounds a little foolish when you say it flatly that way and not piously and slowly from a pulpit or from a retreat director's chair. I suspect it is foolish for many of us. It's foolish for *me* to think about my life in that way, foolish because it removes me from contact with the God who is present in the events of my life.

We should also start with our loneliness and our longing for God. We need to ask him to open our eyes to see, our ears to hear, and our mouths to speak the truth. We long to feel his presence in the work we do, to hear him speaking to us through our imagination, through the people around us. We should start with our strength, our sense of longing. So we also start with our yearning to be with people, to serve, to organize, to enable, to empower, our need to be agents of the rule of God. It is the simple truth that for most of us, clergy or lay, those longings are a real part of

15

why we are where we are, why we run our lives the way we do, why we say the things to our children that we say.

But that passion for the work of God among us is one reason why we are as busy as we are. We know that it is foolish to be so busy that one has no time for oneself. It is stupid to be so busy that one is always tired and worn and still rushing off to the next meeting. That style of life is characteristic of the most inhuman organizations I know of—government and higher education. So we are not talking about that noisy business with which America shouts down its longing for life and hides its emptiness and boredom. We are speaking about the things that need to be done if we are going to be responsibly human in this time. There are many of those things, from working in election campaigns to cleaning up rivers to developing neighborhood health-care organizations. They are all ways in which we join God in his struggle to build with us a livable world out of the chaos and suffering which surrounds us.

The reality is that there *is* little time for regular hours of devotion and meditation. The time we have off ought to be given to sports and relaxation, to partying and silliness, to telling stories and drinking wine. We need to do those things as much as the "serious" work we do. So we are not at the church to spend a "little time alone with the Lord" or to read the Daily Office. We are out and about. We suspect that the conventional piety is really another kind of busyness and we are not sure that, for all its pretension and attraction, it has much to do with the God who is the Lord of history.

The times we find to be quiet and to think are irregularly spaced in the day. The most quiet and solitary time for many individuals is when they are driving the car, off on an errand, picking up someone, going to a meeting, going to work or returning, waiting for someone, jogging, sitting in a bus or train, walking through the city streets. But it is important to recognize the directions in which we are pulled all through our daily existence, torn between what must be done as reasonable, responsible Christians, and the need we have to open ourselves to the presence of God, to attend to that which is not immediately evident or conscious. We need to listen for the Word of God, to attend to his righteous rule, his judgment, his justice, and his claim on us, a claim which he makes by his being: God, and which he makes in his life with us: Jesus Christ, and which he makes in his presence with us: Holy Spirit.

We need and want to be able to feel and know the presence of God, to hear his prayer in our life and know his life in us, and we need also, in God, to get on with the business of living.

I do not believe that medieval spirituality, based in neo-Platonism, is a real option for those of us who live in the present situation. Because it seems to have been the only option that the Church offered, we neglected "prayer." This in turn diminishes our effectiveness as thoughtful and hopeful, active people. We give up listening, praying, mulling over the presence of God in the events of the world and we become distracted, rushing from one thing to another, joining this cause and that— dreaming great dreams only to have them destroyed when things do not come out the way we had imagined. Our personal lives become muddled, we rush off in all directions at once, and we wonder why suddenly we feel defeated by the societal forces we are struggling against. We become manic and depressed at the directions of our lives. Not praying, not thinking carefully in the presence of God is a sure way not to survive the pressures of the modern world. Surely by now, enough people we love have been destroyed for us to realize what the result of thoughtless activism is. This is not just a problem for professionals in the Church. Every man or woman who works hard knows how quickly they lose sight of what they are working for under the pressures of the business world. And those who work at home find that they are so busy doing things *for* the family that they lose touch with the people who are members of the family.

Activism, however, is not necessarily thoughtless and if one becomes aware of the presence of God in whatever it is that one does, it is possible to understand that the situation in which we find ourselves has a definite connection to politics.

If it is true that the only political event in which Jesus participated was his crucifixion, then the life of those who seek to join him in participating in the suffering of the world is going to be a political life. And if participation in that life leads through the world of prayer, then prayer at its heart is also political. The way Israel knew God was in the political events of the life of the people, a *polis*—that is, through political issues and events. One of our mistakes is to think (against our better biblical judgment) that God is no longer active in the lives of a people since the time when the Bible was written. Surely if he was active then, he is active now. One can see a real perception of that activity only occasionally in American life, say, in the Second Inaugural speech of Abraham Lincoln, but it is there for those who have eyes to see. Most of the time we go on as if God had lost an election and given up on the world like a bad loser. When we think about it, we realize that it is not God who has given up; it is we who give in to despair, who fail to discern his presence in the events of history. He is not the one who has to be reminded to be faithful; it is we. It is not God who forgets us; it is we who forget him, as in the prayer, "Lord, if I should forget thee in the midst of things, do not thou forget me."

It is important to remember that the agencies of national domination and exploitation of the world have an investment in the pacification of peoples, in preaching "Peace, peace, when there is no peace." Those who are engaged and concerned for the life of God in the world are dangerous to the establishments and forces of the status quo. These men and women distrust nation-states, especially if they have read the Book of Revelation. They test political statements against what they believe to be real. The deepest reality of the world is God, and the deepest and most important dynamic in the world is love, and love distributed, which is justice. The world is a place for which all humanity must be responsible, it is not something which ought to be used for the profit of particular persons or nations. Christians will also be distrustful of bureaucracy because it so easily takes on a life of its own destructive to the humanity of the people who are administered by it and to the people who administer within it.

The lawyer-theologian William Stringfellow says that if one looks to discern the Spirit of God in the world, one often finds he can tell true events from false events. That is, if a political figure announces that it is necessary to make war in a far-off country because a terrible blow to the national honor would be sustained if war were not made, a thoughtful person might decide that a national honor sustained by the deaths of thousands of persons who have no choice in the matter, or whose honor cannot conceivably be involved, is valueless. The real is the love which pulls people not by might or power, but by its own spirit.

Spirit-filled people are dangerous to nations and establishments of the world because their conclusions spring from premises which are not those of the nations of the establishments.

In a word, persons who believe in God and are active in the life of the world, are dangerous to the vested interests of the world. These men and women do not easily fall for slogans or unexamined assumptions ("We must fight the communist menace in Africa") or racism ("Blacks have lower IQ scores than whites, therefore . . .") or sexism ("Women cannot make rational decisions"). Often those who are close to the life of God in the world do have an uncanny ability to distinguish truth from ambiguity, though not always or inevitably. But when they make mistakes, they bound back to set their faces towards the openings offered by the future. They are dangerous. It is to the best interests of the powerful of the world if persons like that can be made to feel guilty for not displaying conventional piety, or praying as much as believers are supposed to.

It is almost as if we are asked to choose by the political powers: Will you engage in a life of prayer, meditation, and closeness to God in some quiet place, or will you be "mere amateur" political figures, "mere amateur" social workers? We ought to be clear in our own minds that it is an act of political pressure, even propaganda, to ask people to choose between prayer and political life, as it is when we are asked to choose between transcendence and immanence, faith or secularity. These are false choices. As real-life decisions, they have no reality; they are only somewhat useful abstract categories for discussion. The message of the Bible is that God is engaged in the life of the world through his presence in the lives of people, that he is moving this world into the future through his loving care toward unity with him and with all persons. The suggestion that one must choose between God and the world is the presentation of a false choice and is a method by which people are manipulated into losing hope. The loss of hope eventually results in their losing hold of faith and love, or so it is my experience. People who are burdened in this way feel more and more guilty and lost, and come to despair.

In response to the pressures of these false choices between God and the world, we say that the world of spirit and flesh is one because God is one, and our life in the spirit and in the world is one because God is one. I want to suggest as strongly as I can that the tension which is produced by our desire to know God and our desire to serve people is not a tension to be avoided but a tension to be embraced. This tension is none other than the presence of God and we avoid it, cover it up, or choose not to live in it at our risk.

Most Christians feel that tension. We are responsible for what is going on around us and are also responsible for listening to God, for not making judgments or decisions along solely human lines. We know how easily we con ourselves and are conned into self-centered judgments. We know how easily the process of rationalization can lead us into justifying our present easy existence, or into foolishness. The progressive secularization of the world has freed us from superstition and has helped us take responsibility for the future of the world, not as some given inevitability but as a promise toward which we struggle. The notion of the "secular city," the advantages of which are so apparent to us through the growth of technology, has also meant that technology has come to have a demonic life of its own, a life based solely on what is possible and not on human decisions about what is right or best for humankind. The technological culture in which we live seems only concerned for what is, and not with what ought to be; thus questions of right and wrong or even of future consequences are not raised. The development of Third World nations by the great Western powers has resulted in untold suffering, not only because of the exploitation of the poor and the support given to totalitarian "safe" regimes, but also because of the destruction of national pride and native culture sacrificed to the needs of economic development. The situation of these countries is a demonstration of what happens when the depth of the human spirit is ignored, when ancient myths that bind peoples into the universe are set aside as not suitable for industrialized existence. I am suggesting that human beings are complicated creations who are not totally described or ministered to by economic or scientific categories and who are destroyed when what the ancients called the "soul" and what we would call the "whole self" is ignored.

The knowledge people have of themselves, which is not particularly complicated and is made up of their hopes and dreams, is inconvenient knowledge for those interested only in profits and power. We need to pay more attention to that strange, lovely, sometimes terrifying part of us which indicates that the world is not made of mashed potatoes, is not plain and obvious. Materiality, data, things, are not all of life. There is another side to us which is intuitive, communal, poetic, hopeful, dreaming, visionary. We are pulled by two impulses toward idealism and toward pragmatism. We find in ourselves both a prophetic spirit and a priestly spirit, that which says there are things that are right and wrong, and that which says it is important to compromise in order to get things done. One part of us says that we are all individuals, another says we are all part of a common humanity. There is an impulse in us which is "in itself," and an impulse which is "for others." If we ignore either the claims of the inner or the outer reality we are not being fully human; we are not what it means . . . to be a human being. So we are pulled between wanting to listen to the voice of God, to know him, love him, and enjoy him forever, and knowing that the work God wants us to do is feeding the hungry, healing the sick, sheltering the homeless, restoring justice to the ravaged oppressed of the world as their servants. Those impulses are, I think, quite normal and natural, and are based in the life of God himself. The tension between the inner and the outer reality is a gift of God which honors our individuality and our commonality. It is more than that. I think that it is the life of God himself in us.

May they all be one.
Father, may they be one in us,
as you are in me and I in you,
so that the world may believe it was you who sent me.
I have given them the glory you gave to me,

that they may be one as we are one.
With me in them and you in me,
may they be so completely one
that the world will realize that it was you who sent me
and that I have loved them as much as you love me.

As one reads the farewell discourses of Jesus in St. John's Gospel, and especially as one reads the great high-priestly prayer, one is struck by the ambivalence of Jesus' tone. He is one with the Father, yet he has been sent into the world to be with the people. He must leave, he goes to the Father, and his people carry on the work which is his to do.

The tension about which I spoke inheres in this passage. Jesus longs to be one with the Father, to know and love God truly in himself, he longs for peace. One can readily understand this passage when one recalls what Jesus' life was like: constantly being challenged, arguing and debating, surrounded by people who wanted to be healed, meeting needy people who trusted him. In this hectic situation he naturally longs for peace and quiet, yet he knows he belongs with them and belongs to them. It is they to whom he was sent. They are the poor and the suffering and the godforsaken, with whom he is identified. On the cross, he completes this identification, there he is without anything, even, at the end, without a sense of the presence of God. He is truly godforsaken himself as he faces the faceless mystery of death. He is totally engaged in the life of his people, completely identified with humanity, and never more so than in his death.

He loves his friends yet he belongs to the Father. The crucifixion account emphasizes the former as the resurrection emphasizes the latter. Jesus knows somehow the mystery of the presence of the Unknowable in himself, even as he is engaged in the life of the world. He is completely engaged and yet he belongs to an Other, a more complete reality.

There is no way to carry out a spirituality, a life of prayer and meditation, in any other way than as Jesus carried it out, in the world. The two impulses, always for him held together, engagement-and-withdrawal, do not occur alternatively, but simultaneously. There is no way to act out in our lives the life of Jesus except in the places where his life was, in its turn, acted out, in the presence of birth and life and death. So it seems fair to suggest that the appropriate place to center one's life of prayer is the place where Jesus lived, in the struggles and joys of ordinary life, where God is present and where ordinary men and women have always found him.

There is no better place to know God or to be found by him except in the midst of our life, especially as we reflect on the events of our life. There is no better place to be found by God other than in the moments of quiet found in the car or on the subway or in times set aside in the midst of activity. I want to urge thoughtful pauses but I want to suggest that those times of quiet are not more valuable or more holy than the action which surrounds them, which grows out of them and which informs them—the times when we make decisions and listen for the Word of God. Jesus also was constantly aware of the presence of God while he was doing things. He didn't have to go on retreat to listen to the voice of God although he did make retreats before the crisis points in his life, when he was making decisions. But his regular sustaining spirituality was in the midst of action. As he also went aside from time to time to mull things over we also need at times to back off a little. I suggest that the best place to back off is in some place reasonably close to the context of the rest of our lives. A lovely quiet place in the country is a good place to go to relax and we ought to do it, but decision-making and prayer ought to be done within sight of the place where the effects of the decision will be felt and the Word heard in prayer will be lived out.

I once met a former Algerian guerilla who told me it was his discipline to make decisions about terrorist acts while looking at the place and the people who would be affected and to watch if possible the effects of the violence. It was his way of taking responsibility, of feeling the impact of the event in flesh and blood. Few of us are called to such awful and agonizing decisions, but we cannot help but agree that if such decisions have to be made, his was the only ethical way to make them. This model is a useful one; a person who desires to come close to the ultimate reality does that in the context of the totality of his life.

For many of us, the place to which we "retreat" will be the car, the jogging route, or the kitchen table. Those are the places to mull over the events of the day ("meditate" is the classic word) and listen for the Word from God in the events of our lives ("prayer" is the classic word).

So I suggest that as a principle of the spiritual life we give up the idea of going off somewhere, either in our mind or to a "quiet" place, but learn to listen for and hear the ubiquitous voice of God in the events of our lives and, particularly, to embrace the tension of daily life as the appropriate context for decision-making.

Beyond that, the tension between engagement and

withdrawal can be seen to be the same tension which exists inside the Trinity between God the Father (God as he is in himself), God the Son (God as he is utterly engaged in our lives), and God the Holy Spirit (God as he connects the creation with his being itself). The Spirit can be thought of as the connection between God, Wholly Other, and God, Utterly Involved. Tension of this kind indicates the presence of the Spirit. The tension we feel between our need to know God and our need to be involved in the life of the world is the means through which we enter into the presence of the central reality of the universe, God himself.

There are, of course, kinds and degrees of tension which are destructive; there is that terrible and overwhelming *anxiety* which tears people apart. I am referring to a balancing and healthy tension that could be compared to the forces holding a cantilevered beam in place, not the kind of tension which rends and pulls apart. Existing in the tension between engagement and withdrawal means existence "in the Spirit." In this case, to be in the Spirit means to be touched on all sides by the reality of God as Trinity, as revealed in the life of Jesus Christ and communicated to us through the presence of the Spirit. It means we are touched by the presence of the Infinite in the Finite, the presence of the reality of God in the tension which exists at the heart of our personal and political life.

If you don't feel that tension, you may be coming at Christian life and faith in a way which does not give appropriate emphasis to its totality. Perhaps it means that you haven't yet opened yourself fully to the presence of God in history and in the events of your life; perhaps you are praying to a God who is "out there" or are putting on a false face before God, not being honest about your life, perhaps you haven't discovered yet who it is you are. At any rate, I suspect that if you don't feel pulled some way in prayer between withdrawal and engagement, then you ought to reexamine some of your presuppositions.

To put it another way, the tension of which I speak is between the inner and the outer, between the world as it ought to be and the world as it is, between the peace of God and the work of God, between being and doing, the self as self by itself and the self in relationship, between immanence and transcendence. The relationship between these historic polarities is properly tension, one which saves us from the heresy of lonely piety (what we used to call "Jesus and me" piety) and the heresy of political activism and development without human goals and methods (as for example, in Stalinism or capitalist development in the Third World). We are saved from the quietism of not caring, of leaving the world around us to exist in its suffering, and from the nihilism of developing the world regardless of human consequence. To sum up, not to feel the tension which is at the heart of the Christian faith is to lose touch with the reality of God, either by identifying completely with the utterly involved dimension of the being of God or by identifying completely with the transcendent dimension of God.

Insofar as we are in God, we are Israel—the People of the Spirit of God on the road, knowing God in his self and in his presence in the events of history. We are called to act with God in the creation of reality, which to us will always have something to do with truth, decency, honesty, and long-suffering, all ideas which are caught up and expressed in myths and symbols, in stories and songs.

Our life in the Trinity is tested by our ability to discern true events from false events, to see through appearances to reality, to see through ideas to consequences.

During the insurrections in Detroit in 1968, an oral surgeon worked all night in the emergency ward of the Henry Ford Hospital. He took a break and stood smoking at the window of his office, looking down on the city below. It was a horrible sight. Columns of smoke were rising from burned-out houses and stores, there were soldiers on the streets and tanks on the corner. Police cars swept through the streets looking for signs of trouble, and occasionally the surgeon fancied he could hear the rattle of shots off in the distance. Suddenly, to his amazement, he spotted a woman walking through the streets toward the hospital. She was dressed like a suburban matron in the stereotypical Peck and Peck suit, sensible pumps on her feet and a small hat on her head. She made her way down the street, through the smoke, past the tank and the amazed soldiers, straight toward the hospital buildings. A few minutes later, the door to the surgeon's office opened and the woman stood there. She announced that she had driven in from the suburbs and was there, ready for her dental appointment.

This story really happened. Despite our disbelief that someone would be so unaware of the danger, so thoughtless about what was going on around her, confused as we are about whether to admire this woman for her courage for witnessing that life must go on, or shake our heads in disgust that she would be so removed from the life of her city as to attempt to ignore it completely, we have to come to grips with the fact that a woman really walked down a burning street to keep a dentist appointment. So whatever

else we might say about this example, we have in it someone who has chosen a solipsistic reality which we have a
right to suggest may consist only of herself and her needs.
She very likely does not have a heart as big as Noah's ark,
room enough for everyone. One of the problems we have
in praying is that we pray only out of our own needs and
visions and do not reach out to include the totality of
creation. In that sense, our prayer is not political.

True life in God, in the Trinity, is a political life. It is
always an act of resistance to death, and in that context,
prayer and meditation are also acts of resistance to death,
they are as much a saying *no* as a saying *yes*, saying *no* to
that which is false and to which we have decided not to
belong, to have no part in. Prayer—listening for the voice
of God in the life of the world—when it is engaged in
with commitment, ends in the proclamation of the one to
whom we belong, God, and the rejection of the claims of
any other reality, temporal or spiritual.

Spanish people from the Catalonian region have a song
that reflects a prayerful ability to say *no* and proclaims a
sense of belonging that goes beyond the structures of
everyday life and yet reaches out with its own reality.

> Now that we are meeting together,
> We will say what we know,
> And what we often forget,
> We have seen that fear is the law for all of us,
> We have seen that hunger is the worker's bread.
>> No, I say no
>> Let us say no
>> We do not belong to that world.

We have seen that blood that only breeds blood
  is the law for the world
We have seen that men who tell the truth
  are shut up in prison
        No, I say no
        Let us say no
        We do not belong to that world.

Saying *no* is here a statement of belonging and the symbol of a definition of reality. It is a proclamation of the identity of the self which stands by itself and also a proclamation of the identification of that self with a reality in the world which is not the conventional reality which imprisons, shuts up, frightens, and starves.

Prayer is saying *no*. It is saying *no* to the conventional realities of the world and holding oneself ready to be claimed by the Lord, the only God who is God.

We are left where we were, driving to another meeting, feeling the tension of being ourselves and yet involved in the world, feeling the tension of belonging to God in Christ through the power of the Spirit. But we understand that this is just where we ought to be. We aren't fakes, for that which pervades our lives is nothing other than God waiting for us, moving in us, opening doors, eager to help, being for us long before we thought to ask for his grace.

The tension which has been called a sign of our faithlessness is the presence of God himself. We belonged to him before we thought to ask for his acceptance, and we do not belong to the world except in the tension and the anxiety of our lives; we do not belong to the world at all except in and through and with him.

He is the Truth
Seek him in the Kingdom of Anxiety
You will come to a great city that has expected your
    return for many years.

CHAPTER TWO

The World as Haunted Wood

> Lost in a haunted wood,
> Children afraid of the night
> Who have never been happy or good.

W. H. Auden, *September 1, 1939*

How did we get into this mirrored box which keeps us from discovering the gift of God's presence already with us? When I came to pray finally, I wondered how it was that what seemed so apparent now wasn't there before. There are lots of reasons. One might call them, "the excellent reasons for not praying," or "how America defines God out of existence."

I spoke earlier of the political forces which find it useful to keep thoughtful people confused and uncertain of themselves in such a way that they are not as effective in bringing about social change as they ought to be. I wish now to speak of some of the ways in which religious people are manipulated into despair and into a sense of being godforsaken. (Specific ways by which other social groups are manipulated into impotence have been the subject of some excellent sociological work, but Sinnot and Cobb's *The Hidden Injuries of Class* is a splendid example of a study of the demonic forces at work in the lives of working people. Here the discussion is carried on with much the same weight of meaning as I suggest, but using other terms.)

It isn't important whether one thinks that the forces of death in our society are acting consciously or unconsciously. There may indeed be groups of men and women who plan such things and there may also exist demonic powers which, coexisting as they do with structures of goodness in the universe (what we used to call demons and angels) operate in such a way as to destroy the human enterprise.

We used to think that such notions were sick fantasies—five years ago I wouldn't have dared suggest such a thing for fear of being dismissed as a paranoid fanatic—but after the political and economic revelations of the past five years, it seems clear that our worst nightmares come true. In any case, these forces of destruction and death, whether human or inhuman, conscious or unconscious, seem to exist and to exist in powerful ways. Isn't it strange (or providential!) that after a period in which we believed strongly in the possibility of human goodness and the goodness of all "natural" things, we are recalled in such terrible ways to ancient considerations of sin and evil? I have reference, of course, to such phenomena as the Watergate matter, to various conspiracies of business and government, and to the widespread possibility of starvation in the Third World.

The Pauline principalities and powers ("spiritual evil in high places") are still at work and one of the places in which they are most obvious is in the insidious growth of cynicism and nihilism. I come in contact with it, of course, primarily in the educational system and among the young. That which follows does not mean to suggest that nihilism does not exist in other areas of society—in business, family life, and the professions. The person who is caught in the grip of these forces does not pray because he or she has utterly lost hope, sees the material world as the only reality (and that in itself as primeval chaos without meaning or direction), and falls into anxiety, boredom, depression, and decadence.

When, in conversation or a speech, I say something like this, the ordinary response is, "Come off it." Significantly, it is not the response of college administrators, thoughtful observers of the arts (or of television), or parents of college students.

A good example of what I mean can be found in an examination answer written a few years ago by one of my students. The class was asked to discuss the polarities presented as part of the dramatic structure of a Greek play. (The polarities, in case you have ever guessed that teachers don't know the answers to the questions they write, in this trilogy of Aeschylus are light and darkness, freedom and unfreedom, wisdom and arrogant pride, innocence and guilt.) The point of the question was to help students to think through the issues raised in a number of different works and to decide whether those issues are relevant to the problems of our civilization. My student answered the formal part of the question very well and went on, as she should have, to discuss her own response to the problem:

> In the last analysis, polarities of all kinds come down to one basic conflict: Good vs. Evil. Good and evil change sides according to vogue, personality, experience, and subjective whim. Therefore all polarities are saying exactly the same thing: NOTHING. True, they point out different roads or directions which thought or belief can take, yet when faced with the ultimate reduction to simple opposing forces, one knows exactly nothing more than originally except that one is a great deal more humbled and has a peculiar feeling of being lost.
> So a polarity always boils down to the same thing any other polarity is, and nothing is ever achieved in the way of significant answers, by using polarities . . .

One can say that such a statement from the pen of a

young person is merely an instance of nineteen-year-old sophomorism, except that she sums up notions that are honored, if not in words, in action in our national life. Indeed, such statements as "the only thing that counts is what works," "I'd walk over my grandmother for . . ." "winning isn't the important thing, it's the only thing" are grand ideological proclamations made by those who practice every bit of what they preach and more. Beside them, the statement made by my student is sensitive and thoughtful. But it all adds up to the same thing in the end, that is, there is no right or wrong. Since right and wrong are sometimes difficult to discern, they do not exist. Radical relativism is the only option open to us. This is the basis of the twentieth-century creed, whose proudest boast is that it needs no creed. The monster which is alive and well among us is an old beast called nihilism: the notion that right and wrong are meaningless concepts. Nihilism is described precisely by the Italian novelist, Ignatio Silone:

> In its most common aspect, nihilism is the identification of the good, the just and the true with one's own interest. Nihilism is the deep conviction that there is no objective reality behind faiths and doctrines and that the only thing that counts is success . . . nihilism is not an ideology, is not legislatible, is not something to be taken up in school . . . . It is a condition of the spirit, which is judged dangerous only by people who are immune from it or have been cured of it. But most people are not even aware of it, since they think it is an entirely natural way of existence. "Things have always been that way," they say, "and always will be."

Nihilism is a kind of cynicism which refuses to believe in anything, which regards ethical questions as constituting such complicated problems that it is not worth taking the time to consider them . . . it is best to do what is convenient . . . because there is very little possibility that one might reach a satisfying answer. It is true that ethical questions are occasionally quite complicated, but it is also true that one can and must choose. In any case, we are responsible for our choices. Nihilism idolizes the "is" and says that there is no such thing as an "ought." Nihilism lies behind the use of psychotherapeutic techniques to produce "adjustment to society," and behind behavior modification techniques to produce adjustment to prison. It stands behind educational processes which exalt technique and data over significance and meaning. These movements are just as influential in so-called "soft" fields, literary criticism, philosophy, and political science, as they are in more obviously scientific areas such as physics, accounting, and sociology. Thus, nihilistic notions form the background and ideology of the "hidden curriculum" which lies behind the methodology and atmosphere of so much secondary and higher education today.

The roots of twentieth-century nihilism are found in a number of historic events and movements but no idea has been as powerful as the assumption that data is significant in itself. Thus academics have defied the "search for truth" as if truth were something which could be appreciated outside a context, or outside the notion "truth for what." I want to insist that knowledge cannot be acquired outside the conscious or unconscious world of values and feeling.

After a riotous incident involving police, administration, and students, one of the student newspapers at Boston University suggested that the matter be studied by a group which would be called "The Committee to Deal with the Facts" (or CDWF—vaguely, the sound of a club hitting a head). The suggestion was that somehow this committee could discuss objectively what happened that day, leaving aside the interpretations and self-interest of either activist students or administration. The proposal involved the ingenuous idea that somehow the facts would tell the community what was what. Everyone knows that interpretation, perceptions, and previous experience can radically change what people experience as "fact." Since certain facts are always more important to some people that other facts (for instance, the fact that as a policeman you were hit in the head by a brick, or as a student that you were hit in the head by a club) the collection of facts is merely a preliminary to deciding the question of justice—not, what happened, but what ought to have happened? There are no unmodified facts, no facts that are not perceived through a world of values and ethics which are there long before the "facts" become "factual."

The students believed that facts are significant in themselves. On the contrary, I think it is important to insist that facts are always being used by someone for a particular reason. Believing that they are not inevitably leads to frustration and despair. "The facts" is a god that fails. Believing only in the world of data without surrounding that belief with the peculiar (imprecise, intuitive, spiritual) human (or sloshy) values of interpretation— story, myth, vision, symbol—leaves one very much alone in a gritty, flat, boring world. That world is not the one we experience in our deepest selves: indeed, the world of data is as much like the world in which we thrash about from day to day as 2+2=4 is like Moses' vision of a land of milk and honey.

If there is a fact that is not associated with a value, then lack of value becomes a value in itself; it values nothingness, emptiness, loss of hope, and failure of vision. The intellectual moral world in which we live corresponds to what Jesus is talking about when he suggests that if one throws a demon out of a person and does not fill the vacuum with something good, the person is simply being made ready for the arrival of a large number of more dangerous demons. We have thrown out sets of out-of-date values, which supported the vision of the elite, acquisitive and property-owning members of society and which cast certain social classes and castes in subjection to another class, but we have not put in the place of those eighteenth-century values, modern values of communication, community, and corporate decision-making. When inherited aristocracy gave way to what people call meritocracy, we failed to take into account the irrational and societal supports of the so-called meritocrats, who acted as if somehow they really deserved power. They became in the nineteenth century, the new oppressive aristocracy. We have not yet figured out how to come to terms with the reality of such social institutions in a way which does justice to human beings. Instead we have given up the struggle to define value and decided to accept what is—a prescription for the perpetuation of the status quo. We feel empty and are empty. In fact, clergymen report that their most common complaint is that people feel empty and alone.

> Lost in a haunted wood,
> Children afraid of the night
> Who have never been happy or good.

If English, economics, history, or chemistry are to be taught without an understanding of the value implications inherent in their development and teaching, and without an appreciation of the uses to which this learning is going to be put, then perhaps it would be better for the people of the world that they not be taught at all. Our experience with human beings using data without a thoughtful understanding of its place in the spectrum of human experience adds up to a definition of inhuman conduct.

Persons who have been educated in the ordinary American academic institution often find that they cannot pray because they have been subtly indoctrinated with the notion that what is not empirical data does not exist. Promise, vision, hope for a renewed world, subjects about which prayer always seems to speak, are not empirical and therefore, in the mind of American culture, do not exist. In our society, past and future do not exist. That is one reason why we have so few stories to tell our children about the point toward which we think the world and the creation moves.

Have you wondered why commercial television is so boring? Perhaps it is because for it only the present and the empirical exist. It has only the now for its experience; essentially it has no imagination about the past or hope for the future. (Of course, it has programs about the past and even programs, depending on the fad of the moment, about the future. But if you will notice, there is no attempt to portray the characters as they might have been, only a studied attempt to portray them as we are.) In the series "Mary Hartman, Mary Hartman" everything happens on the same emotional level, yesterday does not affect today, and today will not affect tomorrow . . . and therefore the characters respond to a burned cake with the same emotion as to a dying man. Nothing matters.

Just as a playwright friend found his passionate, dreaming, hopeful play turned by a company of sophisticated New York actors into a play about cynical, hopeless people, so all entertainment has become a reflection of the cynicism and hopelessness of the time. The dramatic material is merely preparation for the excitement of the commercial which is the reason why the enterprise exists anyway—to convince people that the only thing that is real, that is truly exciting—is buying things. It comes as no surprise to us that the commercials are more interesting than the programs.

Critics and others wonder why the theatre and other forms of entertainment are depressed. They desperately try to figure out the gimmick in such a play as *Equus*. Why did people pour in to see it? It never occurred to them that perhaps it was not just because it had remarkable staging and direction, that it was cleverly done, but because the play is about the mysterious depths of the human spirit, about dark longings and profound memories, about the search for wisdom. It is precisely because those depths, longings, and memories have been defined out of existence by our nihilist, technological society, yet remain in all their existential and eternal power, that the audience liked *Equus*. They wanted to see this play because they feel the need to satisfy that longing in their hearts which reaches out to the unknown, to that which cannot be quantified. Even in a world which denies the existence of anything except numbers, people reach out to meaning and mystery. "It's too bad these things don't exist, they seem so right."

Vision and passion never grow out of empirical data, which is one reason why some elements in our society have a vested interest in making sure that reality is defined by what can be quantified. Beyond that, there is no use for prayer if there are no real questions of significance, for prayer deals only with significance. Who am I and where am I going? Which of the alternatives should I take? Where lies justice? Why pray if no decisions are to be made, no choices exist, if nothing ought to be because everything only is? Why pray if there is, by definition, nothing to know except what can be counted and if history comes from nowhere and goes to nowhere except for certain economic cycles that tell us nothing about the human response to economic cycles.

In educational institutions the notion exists that all knowledge is equally valuable. That is, getting the facts is what is important, not the uses to which the facts are going to be put. Knowledge is thought of as its own end; it is not a means by which we get to an end. There are no ends, no purposes, which are not equally valuable in this best of all possible economic and educational system. This notion leads universities to lend their facilities to research, the implications of which are destructive to persons. If research means the finding of facts and that all facts are worth finding, then research into better methods of killing (that is, more efficient methods) is just as important as better methods of sustaining life.

Recently, a proposal to gather research data on children

who had an extra chromosome in their gene structure was presented. (Some studies suggested that this condition was present in people who had a tendence to violence). It was proposed that a large population of young persons ought to be investigated; if they were found to have such a chromosome then they would be followed for the purpose of study for the rest of their lives. There seems to have been no thought given to what that might do to produce the kind of despair and rage which would make the thesis of the study self-fulfilling. It goes without saying that the study would have been done in the black community and among the poor. Any study is all right which suggests that violence and the despair from which it grows are biologically produced and are not connected with the social and economic conditions of life. The research study was presented as yet another way of helping the poor cope with their difficulties. Universities were willing to carry out this research, despite its immoral implications, because the consequences were not what they were concerned about, only the acquisition of data (and the funds which the research grant would bring with it).

The same criticism could be made of the proliferation of research institutions whose task is the study of the economic development of "underdeveloped" countries. It doesn't matter to the universities involved that the effect of such research generally is to enrich the elite of those countries and to support the policies of totalitarian governments which remain in power and keep the peace only through terror and wanton oppression. It is simply, to hear the universities tell it, a job which must be done and not a political question in any way. It is not going too far to suggest, on the contrary, that everything the university does is political, or to suggest that everything we all do is political, anything which has to do with the way things are to persons is political—which is precisely why prayer is political at its heart.

At the same time as these studies and institutes go forward, academic institutions wonder why so many of the students who attend them seem to have so little sense of personal morality, so little grasp of ethics. I believe that at least some of the roots of the moral and spiritual disabilities that we suffer lie in the failure of Church and university to take moral stands against economic injustice. The Church should not wonder why so many people find it hard to pray in a cynical world where nothing matters except economic development.

The choice between those who stand for the acquisition of knowledge without significance and those who maintain that all truly human acts involve a choice between right and wrong, however proximate and difficult, is nothing less than a choice between God and the devil. It is a choice between the values of human community, decided no matter how eccentrically, and the values of a faceless society which inevitably deifies its own structure, the status quo.

Why don't persons pray? Why don't they know how to pray? Why aren't they able to see the hand of God in the history of their time and in their own history? One answer is that God has been defined out of the arena of knowledge, and his judgment regarded as a subject not worthy of discussion. We are told that it is no longer an option to believe in the Lord who rules over all nations—he is dysfunctional for the larger American culture. In a world like this, a world with no past and no future, we are indeed alone and afraid, we have no hope. It is entirely reasonable and natural that so many people feel frightened and lonely.

The student whose exam I quoted at the beginning of this chapter suggested that living without a sense of morality left one "humbled." Perhaps a better word would be "humiliated." That is, the proposal that what matters in the world is not human beings, but collections of facts is a notion which treats human beings in a way calculated to humiliate them. We know how people respond when they are humiliated, even if they do not understand the exact mechanism of their humiliation; they are saddened and, sooner or later, enraged. The human wreckage that is the proof of that lies around us in the form of battered children and wives, senseless street violence. I believe that such things are connected to a pervasive nihilism that is more than individual and lies close to the heart of our society.

But nihilism is lived out through individual decisions or lack of decisions. The spectacular nihilism exemplified in the conduct of foreign relations is cozily at home in the heart of the family and in the relations between persons.

When anything goes between two people, when there is no reality beyond sensation or what can be seen and measured, when nothing is either worth doing or not doing, then suddenly we feel worthless ourselves. If everyone does his "own thing," then the possibility of responsibility to or for other people doesn't exist and there is no sense of commonality or community. In the review of a book of pictures celebrating the life of some communards in Vermont, the reviewer notes, "These people are absolutely free, they don't have to do anything for anybody."

Quite a definition of freedom! The gift of freedom from social convention which allows one elbowroom for the self is perverted into the notion that one need not be for others in any way, that one is free to exist solely for the self, unconnected with any other person. O brave new world! In the terms in which I have been discussing the issue, there is nothing to pray about, no decision to be made except to do that which is being done, or that which one feels like doing at the moment. It is a strange freedom, to be enslaved by the self.

As a counselor, I once met with a group of dormitory staff who were vaguely concerned about the life of their building. Everyone in the group insisted that life was really going beautifully there. The meeting went along with an undefined sense of something important not being said until the director could stand it no longer and asked angrily if they lived in the same building as he did. "You say that everything is going well, but I keep sending people home with nervous breakdowns and bailing people out of all kinds of horrendous trouble. Do we live in the same place?"

His words troubled the staff because they thought that the new freedom of life in the dorm—no rules or few rules about conduct—*ought* to lead to happiness and integration of personality, and, therefore, since it *ought* to lead that way, that it *did* lead that way, this despite all the evidence of personal breakdown around them. Finally, one student remarked that he had just finished reading Emile Durkheim's classic, *Suicide*. The book was saying, he thought, that when a group of people don't have some shared system of values, which enables them to hope and to sense bonds of community with others, they lose all hope and the result is suicide. The collective gasp in the room made it clear that he was right on the button. The dorm style was "do your own thing," only no one had stopped to think about responsibility to or membership in the dorm as community, nor had anyone thought much about the development of the I or what it meant when they acted out, "do your *own* thing." The young people in the residence hall had no way to put self and act together, and therefore were acting out of what was there, as if people don't need to *decide* whether or not they will act in certain ways. They *assumed* they knew who they were, as if identity is not put together through a long process of thought and experience. They were, in short, not doing *their* own thing, they were doing whatever it occurred to them to do—which was quite often someone else's own thing, or no one else's own thing. And they were in a state of personal chaos. They had lost a sense of personal significance, which comes from reflection on life and some idea of where one has come from and where one is going. They were living for the moment, not for the future, and, therefore, they had no future. Ultimately human beings seem unable to stand that situation for very long; we cannot bear to be humiliated and lost.

The decision for death is made in all sorts of ways. Students (and their parents) drink too much, seeking to drown out the longings and the hopes which call them beyond the moment, they smoke too much dope, end up not going to class, not taking any responsibility for local or national politics. These are all signs of death. They believe neither in themselves nor in others. The individual moments of their lives come to be without coherence or organization and stretch in a meaningless line on to a death which all too often comes sooner rather than later. We have become people who are simply acting out the roles that society has said w   ought to live, not roles we have chosen. We are the ha   y-go-lucky rich Americans of the late twentieth century.

Silone again:

> It is nihilistic to make sacrifices for a cause one doesn't actually believe, although one pretends to. It is nihilistic to exalt courage and heroism independently of the cause they serve, here the nihilist equates the martyr with the mercenary.

Since they have no other way to judge, students do not know whether the sacrifices they and their parents are making for them to go to college makes them martyrs or mercenaries. They do not know why they should go to college except that it *should* enable them to get better jobs and make more money. Actually, the atmosphere of most universities, almost despite itself, breathes another unspoken purpose for their being there, that is, the discernment of the reality which lies behind the appearances of the world, the discovery and elucidation of the ways people have come at making sense out of the world. In the end that does not have much to do with anyone getting a better job or making more money. And since that visionary way of looking at education is not available to students, having been defined out of existence by our nihilist culture, students and their parents are confused and disoriented by higher education, and the university itself is chaotic and torn apart by lack of clarity as to its purpose.

Not just in colleges but throughout America the nihilist atmosphere leads to boredom and depression, and depression leads to attempts to make the time go by through seeking sensation. It is as part of this process that we end up with the amateur-hour decadence of the college and the suburbs today. While we experience nothing comparable to the boredom and decadence of the eighteenth-century aristocrat, if we carry on long enough, perhaps we will gain the skills necessary to bury ourselves in the strangely bitter sweetness of decadence. In any case, the decadence of our time has the same roots as that of the eighteenth century, the depression which comes to an elite which do not believe in anything, does not have the ability to give life or to accept real gifts of life from others. We think everyone and anything can be bought, including ourselves. The economic, political and intellectual development of our country has led us to this spiritually death-dealing situation.

We are not the first nation to place ourselves in this situation:

See what days are coming—this is the Lord Yahweh who speaks—a day when I will bring famine on the country: a famine not of bread, a drought not of water, but of hearing the word of Yahweh. They will stagger from sea to sea, wander from north to east, seeking the Word of Yahweh and failing to find it. (Amos 8: 11-12)

Americans wonder why it is that prayer comes hard when they have been immersed in that cultural background all their lives, a background which wishes to repudiate in every way the possibilities suggested by prayer, the possibility, chiefly, that human nature can be changed and the world be recreated into a humanly livable place. So we find all sorts of people resorting to tricks and fancy theories which are supposed to make belief easier. But the gimmicks of the gurus fade in and out of fashion while the real world, with its real evil and its real threat, increasingly carries with it the notion that the enterprise of human endeavor, the idea that one might change one's life and participate in the groaning struggle of the world as it seeks to come to life, is a hopeless and dead-ended enterprise. Our society, mired in nihilism, teaches that life is a difficult and ultimately despairing thing, that things and people do not change, that one cannot change except in ways which make acceptance of the present situation of corruption and debilitating anxiety easier to bear. It is easier to learn a method of meditation, which enables one to survive in the midst of the mad struggle for success, than it is to understand that the struggle for success is a death-dealing enterprise which ought to be resisted by men and women who will say that they do not and will not belong to it. Our culture in its groovier forms also suggests that if one cannot bear the terrible rat race of the world, one ought to seek surcease in physical sensation. I agree that one might and could be open to all sorts of experience, but insist that our experiences and energies ought to be *focused* on the strengthening of ourselves for the struggle against oppressive and exploitative powers.

Is it too much to say that the single most pervasive message of American capitalist society is that the chief end of man is to sit down, drink beer, and watch men who are paid to hit each other do it, and to bet whether one group of men will do it so much better than another group of men that they will win a game called professional football?

I sound like a spoilsport. Worse than that, I'm beginning to sound like a puritanical minister. I can hear my friends saying, "Let's not hit out at football *and* encounter groups in adjoining paragraphs." Everyone is sick, with good reason, of the Mrs. Grundys of the world, and as I have made clear before and will make even clearer later, I am far more in favor of a life which says *yes* than one which says *no*, far more interested in affirming signs of grace and goodness than I am in sniffing out evil. The one thing my analysis leaves out in all of the above is the powerful and self-willed work of the Spirit through persons in our time. Movements for personal and national liberation have grown up all over the world. They are not evenly thoughtful or ethical; the one thing they have not done is fall into what is our national temptation, to let it all go, nihilistically to say that nothing matters, to act, as Harvey Cox suggests we not act, as if nothing is of any use and we ought to leave it to the snake. All over the world men and women have not given up on the human struggle, which I believe is a result of the activity of God working in and through the events of history and coopting human cooperation in that activity.

I think it is time to reaffirm our intent to oppose chaos and hopelessness through the Word of God. And I wish, therefore, to speak of love, not the love of the movie magazines which is idolatry, or the love of television which so transitory, but the love which Dosteovsky described when he said that love in action is a harsh and dreadful thing compared to love in dreams. I am speaking of love in the world of flesh informed by the love of the Spirit. This is the love which survived being forsaken and lost and which was nailed to the cross, which survived and defeated death, just because it is worldly and realistic in spirit and body.

Our society has defined real prayer out of existence, and put in its place pagan prayer, the prayer of beggars and slaves. But we are citizens of another country and our prayer is essentially to hear that prayer which God directs to us, which leads into the future. The historical accident of the development of spiritual theology in the Church has made prayer something which can only take place away from the events of history, or which affects only an individual praying in the midst of history but not connected with it. It is high time to restore the scriptural prayer which seeks the will of God on earth as in heaven.

I wish to speak here then of a prayer which equips men and women to be even more resistant to death than they imagined they could be, a prayer which takes as its main category the will of God acting through the cooperation of his people. This prayer turns us to the identification of the powerful structures of good existing around us, structures which have the potential to change us from the inside out and the outside in. I speak then of prayer emanating from the Word of God in our midst, our neighbor in Christ, coming to us from the tensions which we feel and leading us into a future the beauty of which we can only vaguely apprehend.

In the face of death, live humanly, in the middle of chaos, celebrate the Word. Amidst babel, I repeat, speak the truth. Confront the noise and verbiage and falsehood of death with the truth and potency and efficacy of the Word of God. Know the Word, teach the

Word, nurture the Word, preach the Word, defend the Word, incarnate the Word, do the Word, live the Word. And more than that, in the Word of God, expose death and all death's works and wiles, rebuke lies, cast out demons, exorcise, cleanse the possessed, raise those who are dead in mind and conscience. (William Stringfellow, *An Ethic*)

It is no exaggeration to say that we live among a people who are in danger of being dead in mind and conscience and who desperately need to be raised from that death. But the first persons we ought to raise from the death of mind and conscience are ourselves.

In that day I will re-erect the tottering hut of David and make good the gaps in it, restore its ruins and rebuild it as it was in the days of old, so that they can conquer the remnant of Edom and all the nations that belonged to me.
It is Yahweh who speaks, and he will carry it out.
The days are coming now—it is Yahweh who speaks—when harvest will follow directly after plowing, and treading of grapes soon after sowing, when the mountains will run with new wine and the hills all flow with it.
I mean to restore the fortunes of my people Israel; they will rebuild the ruined cities and live in them, plant vineyards and drink their wine, dig gardens and eat their produce.
I will plant them in their own country, never to be rooted up again out of the land I will have given them, says Yahweh, your God.

(Amos 9:11)

CHAPTER THREE

The World as Our Flesh

> *He is the Life*
> *Seek him in the world of the flesh*
> *And at your marriage all its occasions will*
> *dance for joy.*

W. H. Auden, *For the Time Being*

William Stringfellow suggests that our first task is to raise up those who are dead in mind and conscience. Who are they? Do not take it amiss if I use you for an example, dear reader, or rather use half of you, the men. I want to talk about the *person* who exists in the context which was described in the last chapter, the context in which God has been defined out of existence, and cynical nothingness enthroned in his place. Since it is useful to look at figures somewhat removed from specific individuals, but not useful to get so far away from living persons that what you are talking about is merely an abstract idea, I thought it would be best if we chose an image of humanity which, at least for half of us, is well known. Since there has been a great deal written about women and the role of women, maybe it would be good for us to make a beginning by writing about men. A disclaimer: in writing about the male image, I do not intend to deny the importance of writing about women or the importance of looking at humanity from the point of view of the identity of roles, androgyny. I think you will see that I end up somewhat closer to the latter than to some macho idea of male. In any case, there are some useful tools around to help us get some idea of what it is to be a "man," and it is high time some of us thought seriously about that.

When I finish a description of "male," I want to use that figure to talk about the praying person, that is, about what is required before one begins to pray, and to use this

59

chapter as a way to self-knowledge. To discover and to choose one's own self is the necessary beginning of all prayer; it's what you have to know first, not as complete knowledge, or fully developed, but as choice. That is, we must, however feebly, find ourselves before finding the God who has already chosen us and who brings us by his grace to the ability to say *yes* to ourselves, revealing himself as the one who has led us to ourselves, the one who in the beginning began the process by which we struggled to know ourselves.

> Our desire and our prayer should be summed up in St. Augustine's words: *Noverim te, noverim me.* (May I know you, may I know myself.) We wish to gain a true evaluation of ourselves and of the world so as to understand the meaning of our life as children of God, our Father and Redeemer. (Thomas Merton, *Contemplative Prayer*, p. 67)

As foil for the discussion of male, which is the way by which I will come at a definition of ourselves, I will use the work of two famous clowns, Charles Chaplin and Woody Allen. The contrast between them will demonstrate to us something of what has happened to the image of male in the modern world and therefore something of what has happened to men in relation to their self-image.

I use clowns because they are magic figures, that is, they stand for hopes and dreams lifted out of life, exaggerated. They throw into high relief the subject about which they are clowning, emphasizing only one or two aspects of the person or the situation, just as an item of clothing or a way of walking stands for a whole character or a whole way of being. For our purposes, that is exactly right. We want to ask them what are the special characteristics of "male" in the periods in which they worked and work.

Clowns adopt persona which exist as story, which are, therefore, larger than life, and as comic persona or story-person, they show us what it is about ourselves that we find absurd. A clown demonstrates what it is we are suspicious of in ourselves, what we don't somehow like without quite knowing why, what we are in the process of separating ourselves from, disavowing. Whatever is funny about us is acted out by clowns such as Chaplin and Allen. They are innocent figures without innocence, devoid of anything save some few aspects of character (This is one reason why they are frightening to children who expect them to be human when they never can be. This is also one reason why Allen is frightening to some of us, who begin to wonder if it is a role or the totality of the person). So a clown is deliberately inhuman as "clown" but the trick of his theatrical presence gives us clues into what is behind the defenses of the persons being clowned at.

We do not laugh at the clowns. With us as partner, the clowns laugh at us, portraying us in our weakness, cupidity, stupidity, selfishness, and failure. The joke at the circus is always on you or on someone sitting behind you with the same name as you. Surely one of the reasons the children laugh so much at the clowns (once they get over their fear of seeing a fantasy creature come to life) is because the clowns make it possible for them to laugh at adults, that is, at their parents, something which is either not possible or difficult in the family context. The clown is a caricature of some aspect of our humanity. One notices immediately his single-mindedness and lack of complexity and that is why Chaplin and Allen have chosen very specific aspects of the human situation to clown around.

Chaplin is without doubt one of the great figures of the first half of the century. As clown he used the economic structures he was making fun of to distribute and popularize his making fun of them. The main character, Charlie, the waif, is an upside-down successful businessman. He dresses the same way as the model businessman, bowler hat, striped pants, wing collar, tail coat, malacca cane. Somehow though, things don't fit just right, everything isn't quite as it seems, but that's right to the ironic point. Charlie is hardworking, honest, eager to please, everything Horatio Alger said you should be if you were going to be successful, but unlike an Alger hero, things never go right for Charlie. He is always being put down or put out, chased and beaten by the true businessman who is greedy, mean, and narrow. Chaplin mocks the whole idea of the businessman as the pillar of society. He has all the moral characteristics that a pillar of society is supposed to have, but he never reaches success, while the people in his movies who do reach success have exactly the opposite characteristics. It makes you think. Or, at least, it was supposed to make you think.

While Charlie is lovable as all hell, he is a dismal failure in the eyes of the world. Chaplin films say clearly, in contrast to the American myth, good hard-working people are not successful, their virtues are not what are rewarded, Horatio Alger is the bunk. Charlie demonstrates the falseness of a success ethic based on hard work and honesty. He totters down the street, waving his cane, straight into another disaster, saying with every bone and muscle in his body, "What they say about life isn't true."

Many viewers in the thirties got the message. The reason they were down-and-out was not because they were lazy and dishonest, bad people. It was because the world was upside down, lazy and dishonest persons were in fact the successful ones. That was good news in a depression-ridden country, where the business of the country was business, the definition of respectability. In many ways this message has always been good news:

He has shown the power of his arm,
he has routed the proud of heart.
He has pulled princes from their thrones and exalted the lowly.
The hungry he has filled with good things, the rich sent empty away.

(Luke 1:51-53)

Chaplin was a political man, who knew exactly what he was doing in those films. That is evident not only in his great anti-Hitler film, *The Great Dictator*, but all through his work. It is clearest in *Modern Times* where the industrial technology of the period is made fun of just because it is so utterly inhuman that it is clearly absurd for anyone to think that human beings will put up with it. The boobs who would think of such things as an automatic feeding machine (so a man would not have to take a lunch hour in order to eat) are justifiably and mercilessly made fun of because they have ignored common sense and decency in their greed for profit.

In Chaplin's films, the rich usually even look terrible. Their faces reveal their profound unhappiness, their grounding in mindless greed. On the other hand, the poor are sweet and open in appearance, they are pure in heart, kind and good. They are what the scriptures call "the quiet in the land."

Chaplin mocks the capitalist entrepreneur, the businessman of the twenties and thirties. He clowns around the superego, making fun of false respectibility, fake order rooted in chaos, filthy cleanliness. He shows that the success-based morality promoted in the capitalist culture is absurd and serves only the purposes of the wealthy and powerful. At the same time that he scorns conventional respectability, he honors sincerity, decency, simplicity, and warm human love.

Chaplin helped people to survive the depression by pointing out the forces arrayed against them and suggesting that the pretense to respectability of the rich and powerful was based on a lie. He demonstrated in film after film the hollowness of cultural values which said that hard work and honesty would lead to success and wealth. Chaplin suggests that dishonesty, meanness, and hatred are what lead to success, and he associates them in his films with unhappiness, boredom, and general misery. We don't need a Chaplin in our time; we have Watergate.

The image we have of ourselves in the latter part of the seventies is in considerable contrast to that of the twenties. In the fifties and sixties, many of us gave up on the notion of success and respectability, except as a continuing unconscious hangup and adopted a private vision of ourselves as fathers and lovers. That is, the values of success were questioned in a number of popular books and films of the time (*The Lonely Crowd, Executive Suite,* etc.), and an individualist image of self as family man or lovable jock (Robert Young/Burt Reynolds) arose, as it were. A man was thought to be successful if his family "turned out well." I'll never forget a Detroit funeral director telling me that while he wasn't a terribly religious man, he did occasionally stop into a church to pray for his family. Grateful only that he wasn't praying for increased business (which was itself significant!), I didn't stop to question him about his extraordinary household god which was concerned to make sure everyone got into good colleges. But whether we like it or not, my funeral director was the prototype of the image of male in the fifties or sixties. The good family man was completely concerned about his children and their well-being, and was busy building and planting those spectacularly neat and green suburbs which produced the hippies of the late sixties.

His mirror-image was the Playboy, equally successful, only on a one-to-one level (or one-to-one-to-one-to-one). Still and all, the Playboy took good care of his bunny and even spent long hours philosophizing about it so as to make sure he didn't feel guilty over what he seemed to feel enormously guilty about.

The sixties put the boot to the dreams of the family man. First of all, no one's children turned out the way they were supposed to; they did not carry on the image their parents would have been more than happy to give them. The generations turned out unable even to make sense to each other in conversation. Beyond that, boys, for example, grew their hair (as long as *girls*), smoked dope, and lived with women or men out of wedlock. They vowed not to acquire things aimlessly, and raised their children *with* other people's children in communes. From the point of view of the man of the fifties, they were a disaster, which is what the young people meant what they were doing to mean. Inside, many of those rebellious hippies and communards of the late sixties were burghers waiting to be released from their parents long enough to be born, but generally their style from that day to this has been to deny the hopes and dreams of their parents' generation.

Beyond that, the social supports of respectable life broke down, Government was no longer thought of as a protecting friend. Indeed, the government, through various means, seemed bent on attacking men and their hopes. Children were sent to war, arrested for smoking pot, attacked for demonstrating, and bused across town for the purpose of integration. A world which the father organized for the protection of his children seemed bent on attacking him through attacking them. The family as an institution seemed to be falling apart.

We know how far men have come to question themselves in the work of Woody Allen. Allen mocks the male ego. He makes fun of the seducer, the cool, sophisticated man of the world, the confident, fatherly authority figure, the successful entrepreneur. Allen makes fun of the ego in much the same way as Chaplin made fun of the superego. Allen tells the dirty little secret that all those men who embody the jock are really frightened poseurs inside— really little boys who are whistling in the dark. If inside each small insecure Woody Allen there is a jock waiting to be let out, it is also clear that inside each jock there is a Woody Allen waiting to be acknowledged. Allen's popularity shows that people believe this to be true. Try, if you will, to hold the images of Hugh Hefner and Woody Allen together in your mind. See what I mean? The two images cannot exist together, Allen blows Hefner away. He shows up Hefner's shallowness, his insecurity, his self-love, and his falsity. In *Play It Again, Sam,* Allen imitates Humphrey Bogart while stumbling and crashing through his apartment in his self-imposed role of seducer of a girl who already loves him as he is. When he is himself, that is, vulnerable, she loves him more.

Peter Seller's detective, Clouseau, an incredibly clumsy man, also mocks the tough private eyes of the films of the past. Significantly enough, the audiences identify with Allen and Sellers, not with the hard-nosed loners of the films of the past.

The problem of discovering a male image is not exclusively modern. Though one ought to be careful about seeing easy ancient parallels to modern problems, Euripedes' *The Bacchae* may reveal an ancient approach to what happens to the male who wears a false macho mask. (No one seems *ever* to have thought that there could be a *real* macho type.) In the play, the effeminate god of wine, Bacchus, comes to Thebes, which is ruled by Pentheus, a boy-king. Bacchus's purpose is ostensibly to avenge a slight, —Pentheus and his family have denied his divinity. The boy, who rules as he thinks a king ought to rule, that is, in an obviously over-compensating, "masculine," authoritarian way, is tricked by the god into lowering his defenses. The god takes him in an intoxicated, highly aroused state to the place where his mother and sisters are observing the rites of Dionysius. There he is revealed to be a male dressed in women's clothes, and he is killed by his own mother. Our last image of him alive, in a heart-rending narrative spoken by the inevitable messenger, is as a boy screaming, "Mummy, it's me," to his unhearing, maddened mother. Boys, says Euripedes, ought not to pretend to be men. Men ought not to pretend to an image that is not themselves, says Woody Allen.

The absurdity of the pretentious, swaggering male image and the failure of our culture to produce sensitive, recognizably human male images leads one to wonder why there is not more homosexuality than less. It is this man, the one who tries to act out the culturally accepted role, that Allen mocks. What he is making fun of is the mask of male ego, mocking the assumption that men are in control of their relationships and revealing underneath the chaos, loneliness, and pretense of the little boys who have never grown out of their dependency into adulthood. "Mummy, it's me," they still cry to the warm little bunnies who wait on them.

Chaplin used a new medium, whose basic technique is light shining through (film) to show the cracks and crevices of a society; Allen uses the same medium to demonstrate the weakness and falseness of the male ego-image.

Growth of interest in women's liberation and concern about what it means to be a female has left men at a serious disadvantage in the battle of the sexes. Women have *actually thought about* women's liberation, and have discovered exemplary women who lives are available as models for women of different ages. Men have a hard time finding a man to be proud of. Other than macho-imposters, there are few men around to identify with. Who really wants to be like Richard Nixon, Hugh Hefner, Henry Kissinger, John Wayne, or Vince Lombardy? The new breed of male actors gives us some vague notions of what might be the new male model—Paul Newman, Jack Nicholson and Robert Redford come to mind, but not all of us are *that* handsome, if you know what I mean.

As I travel I find it instructive to listen to men ordering women around airport and train stations. Women seem to be in charge of everything, the luggage, the children, the passports. The male role and major task seems to be to stand around complaining and shouting out ill-tempered orders which no one takes seriously. Men seem really convinced that women must do as they say. Understandably, but unfortunately, women fall into the easiest way to handle the situation; they pretend the man is in control. "Mummy, it's me."

The image of man is an indistinct shadow; the false ego is something men hide behind and which prevents their growing into adulthood. There is no better witness to this tragedy than Virginia Woolf. She writes (in *A Room of One's Own*) of the male writer who is so concerned to assert his male ego that he cannot, in fact, write about anything else. More especially, he is unable to write about women. She tells how she respects the male ego for its direct self-confidence, but ultimately and unfortunately:

> I am bored. But why was I bored? Partly because of the dominance of the letter "I" and the aridity, which, like a giant beech tree it casts in its shade. Nothing will grow there. And partly for some more obscure reason. There seemed to be some obstacle, some impediment of (the author's) mind which blocked the fountain of creative energy and shored it within narrow limits.

Men have a hard time praying partially because self-identity is hard to arrive at for men, because male models and roles do not lead to real prayer which is based in the real self. Praying like that, says Thomas Merton, is like trying to walk without feet. The man who prays must be ready to listen, not always to be the initiator. The one who prays for reconciliation must be ready to think over the past, be ready to admit wrong. The one who prays trusts God and his acts in history and doesn't depend solely on himself. He must be ready to ask for help, willing to admit his needfulness and pray out of it. Contemporary models, which are confused, are not helpful to the man who comes to pray.

So men must begin to give up the old macho penile myth and begin to develop a new myth of what it means to be a man. And if objections can be raised that this is really too much to expect, that men at this stage of history will never reject the idea of male which has been held out as desirable for centuries, then attention must be drawn, first, to the expectation that God will make all things new and second, to a specific historical sign of that in China, where in the past twenty years men have had to reconstruct their relationship with women from the ground up. This was done primarily by recognizing that the position of women had been that of slaves, and by then allowing women to confront men with their feelings about this, that is, making it possible for them to "speak bitterness," and then monitoring the response of men to women's situation through group interaction and criticism. The process was and is neither easy nor perfect, but it has achieved considerable success, perhaps because it allowed the people to deal with the problem on the grass-roots level, that is, in terms of daily life in the village.

There are signs in our culture that the male image is doing us more harm than good. In short, it is time, if our nature is obnoxious and destructive to us, to change our

nature. The old image has fallen apart in front of our eyes
(on the movie screen) and such an unlikely person as
Woody Allen has trampled it under his saddle shoes. Indeed, it is stumbling, clumsy, weak, needy, frightened
little Allen who, these days, gets the girl! How sensible
women have become.

We began with trying to figure out what it is, anyway,
"to be a man." The one thing we can no longer accept is
the given cultural definition of male, for neither the successful Victorian businessman, nor the pragmatic family-
oriented organization man, nor the playboy will meet our
needs for authenticity.

Beyond that, for all Christians, men and women, the
theological problem is complicated by the Church's historic suspicion of the ego, and by the way religious institutions retard personal growth by keeping people dependent on a false image of God as the all-powerful, im-
mutable One before whom one must disappear. We must
find a way to understand the humanity of God among us,
and at the same time recover some notion of the proper
dignity of the ego and the relationship of ego's needs to
God's demands.

The Neo-Platonic tradition in prayer has denigrated our
particularity in the same way as the contemporary
technological society has denigrated our commonality.
Some spiritual systems suggest that the proper aim of faith
is the destruction of the ego, seeing ego of any kind and
not alienated sinful ego as inevitably opposed to the will
of God. Too often the humility of the creature before the
creator has been defined in terms of the extinction of ego. I
want to suggest that it is only before God that we can truly
be the individual we are, truly, that is, the ego we are.

And, far from rejecting ego, looking to the growth of ego in community is the task toward which the Lord urges us. Theologically speaking, we say that we do not walk the middle way between person and the All, we are committed to personality.

In the last chapters of St. John's Gospel, Jesus bids farewell to his disciples in what is called the High Priestly Prayer. He speaks of himself in relationship to the Father and uses the word "I" thirty-three times. The word stamps its way down the pages and we sense that this is neither a man erecting a monument to his sexuality, a monument behind which he wishes to hide, nor bent in humility before an annihilating presence, but a man affirmed and authentic. He is, in the words of Kierkegaard, being himself in the presence of God, not defining himself in terms of a societal image, but as one in relationship. He is obedient son, obedient in his own way, in his own time, to one who shares his existence with him, who is open and vulnerable.

One of the worst mistakes religious people have made is to suggest that we must destroy ourselves before God. It is inappropriate self, self-out-of-control, self-worshipping self, which must be examined and rooted out. That is the self which builds its happiness on the misery of others; the racist, sexist, exploitative self. The self which is obedient to the demonic forces standing behind the television image of humanity, telling us that we are defined by our clothes, our car or cigarette or job is replaced by authentic being. It is that old self which is needful but not admitting it, resentful but not acknowledging it, which ought to be left behind. The true self, the self for which Christ gave up his life, stands proudly before God as his creation, his child, his partner in the work of rebuilding the earth and human society under the rule of God. It is this self which suffers crucifixion at the hands of the evil forces of the world. The resurrection means that we speak to God as the I we are and the I we know we are becoming with his help, the I God prays into existence. That I is the one we are so afraid of being, because it is an I created as act of faith before God, but it is also the I we need so much to be.

God does not love us because we are lovable, he loves and loves us and, finally, we become lovable in response to his love. It is that I which is the self as it faces death, the enemy we must all face alone. In Christ, the ego is restored to sonship, for it is only that new I which can pray, which has the strength to listen and to cry for help.

One of the ways through which we discover the self we are before God is to tell a story about ourselves. We define the self in relation to history by seeing ourselves not as audience but as actors on the stage of history. We come to that understanding by mulling over for ourselves where we have come from and where we hope to go. Another way of saying it is that we find our ego when we are able to articulate our past and project a vision of the future. We ask, what has made me what I am, what kind of person do I hope to be? One of the ways of getting at the reality of our individuality and identity is to attempt to tell our story prayerfully to God. It is sometimes helpful to ask these questions in the presence of God. "How is it to be the person I am? How will it be if I become the person I want to be?"

If I am a person who has learned slowly and painfully how to relate to people in a way that *seems* easy and confident, but which is really not so down deep, it is good for me to share that honestly with God and hope that one day I might grow into a person who genuinely and authentically can reach out to others and allow others to reach out to me. If I am another person whose relationships with people are crippled and made difficult by some past history, either personal or ethnic, it is good for me to share *that* with God and hope and pray for a spiritual gift which will allow me to reach through the barriers surrounding each one of us. In this way, we come from the people we are to grow toward the person we want to be before God.

In just this way, we learn to speak our own name, we learn who it is, this self we are. When we have some understanding of what it means to be that person— ourselves—we are hearing God call our name. We know whom it is that he addresses, and whom he calls to grow even more. When we know that from which we came and that to which we hope to go, we write our own myth in the same way that all peoples have their myths. Our personal myth is just as precious, potentially as life-giving, as myths of national and tribal selfhood. Our myth can lead us to selfhood, to rediscovery of the self. The satisfaction of that need to be secure in our own identity can save us from the demons which plague our national life, sensation seeking and consumerism as approaches to identity, and serve as the answer to the problems of boredom and depression.

I suggest that prayerful recapitulation of our history and prayerful projection of our future are ways of coming alive. If we are the animal that knows it must die, we must become friends with time and the movement of time so that we can see ourselves inside the process of time, not as lost and alone, but in our uniqueness among friends. We are lost and alone in the history of things until we see ourselves as the persons we are—not walking penises in the case of men, but persons active in history and prayerfully awake to the Word of God in our own time. We find in the events of our history the Lord of all history, and we find, sometimes to our great surprise, that he is ours and we are his, now and forever.

He is the Life

Seek him in the world of the flesh

And at your marriage all its occasions will dance for joy.

CHAPTER FOUR

Voices from the Imagination

Robert: How do you mean, voices?
Joan: I heard voices telling me what to do.
Robert: They come from your imagination.
Joan: Of course, that is how the messages of
God come to us.

George Bernard Shaw, *St. Joan*

One of the ways to become more aware of the presence of God is to train ourselves in the expectation of his presence. Knowing God and being known by him is more than a habit, but it is at least that. It means ordering our lives so that we expect God to touch us and change us; it means ordering whatever situations and routines we can so that we are conscious, alert, and ready to hear the voice of God speaking from our unconscious through our imagination. George Bernard Shaw might not spring to mind as a writer to turn to for spiritual advice, but there is a profound insight in a passage from *St. Joan.* Joan is being questioned by one of her captors:

Robert: How do you mean, voices?
Joan: I heard voices telling me what to do.
Robert: They come from your imagination.
Joan: Of course, that is how the messages of God come to us.

One of the ways in which we come close to the presence of God is in listening to the voices of our imagination. More often than not, God is waiting for us to open the door and allow him to speak, to lead us to ourselves and to the changes and decisions we know we must make and which we have been avoiding. But if we cultivate the sense of readiness, an openness to events and conversations, God may be discerned as he reaches out to us and leads us to reach out to those around us. In this way, he teaches us over and over again of the ever-renewing wonder of his graciousness and gives us his gift: the future.

For example, one winter I took a few days to hole up with some former students who were living in Woods Hole, Massachusetts. Since they were busy about their lives, I had a good deal of what I was looking for, time for myself. It was a time to think and to try to pray, which I was learning to do rather painfully and stumblingly, not knowing quite where to look or what to do.

The day I was to return to Boston, I got up very early in the morning to catch a bus down in the little town. I crept out of the house, having said good-bye the night before. A light snow was falling through the street lamps and since the house was on a hill overlooking the town, I could see through the snow the lights of the research vessels and ferryboats in the harbor. The air was full of that sound that only falling snow makes and you can only hear in the country where there is no traffic. I could also hear the romantic and peculiar sounds of a small harbor, lapping water, creaking ropes, boats moving restlessly in their berths, eager to be back where they belong, on the open sea. It was indescribably lovely: there was a kind of luminous clarity to it. Then the swish of the snow, the crunch of my boots on the pavement, the sounds of the sea and its creatures were joined by a kind of gentle ringing, a chiming.

How can I tell you how it was. I stopped and stood under a lamp and listened to this musical sound and thought, "My God, I'm having a religious experience." As you can imagine, I wasn't exactly prepared for such an eventuality and was about to suggest to God that he arrange to come to me in a few months when I would be better prepared. Like Abraham, when he was first called by God, I felt that God had made a mistake, surely he was seeking someone else on that block, he couldn't mean me. For a moment I was stunned and just stood there, waiting.

I discovered then that the sound came from a wind chime hung on one of the porches along the street, left out by mistake from the summer. Its glass strips, moving gently in the light wind, rang a little at first and then pulsed into full chime. It was not the voice of God, at least not formally. But the voice of God came to me, as it always has, not in the spectacular, not in the fire, the earthquake, or the ringing chime on a winter morning, but later on the bus. Then there came the still small voice which spoke through my imagination. It was a voice I had ignored even as I obeyed its calling me back to Boston, back to the university.

I don't know Who—or what—put the question, I don't even know when it was put. I don't even remember answering. But at some moment I did answer *Yes* to Someone—or Something—and from that hour I was certain that existence is meaningful and that, therefore, my life, in self-surrender, had a goal. (D. Hammarskjöld, *Markings*, Whitsunday, 1961)

Hammarskjöld puts it better than I, but I suspect that he sums up the experience of many people who hear the voice of God speaking the things they do not expect to hear, maybe do not want to hear, or do not think they are worthy to hear. It is unmistakable because it is at once so human and so beyond all humanity. It is a voice which honors the tension between the God who speaks and the God who remains in silence.

I don't think I even thought some of those things at that time, but later I knew that that moment had been a turning point, not because of a silly romantic misunderstanding about the wind chime, but because I took that moment to be what it was — rather, I let that moment be what it was. God does not speak in wind chimes, he speaks in us, and with us and through us as he spoke in Jesus Christ and as he speaks in the mouths of our brothers and sisters all over the world. But the wind chime can show us how foolish we are to expect him to act in ways other than the miraculous ways he acts in us. Karl Barth says somewhere that God does not become thunder, he becomes man, and it is to humanity that we must turn with a lively expectation of hearing the voice of God.

Boston University, where I work, rejoiced in the reputation of having one of the most difficult student bodies in the country during the great period of student activism. We were proud of that reputation for passion and commitment and still are, even though that may seem strange to people who didn't know the universities or us during that time. It was, to put it mildly, the best of times and the worst of times, and we who went through it are marked by it for better and for worse for the rest of our lives. One spring we were in the midst of the usual crisis and were holding a rally in the chapel, the only neutral ground which could accommodate a large number of people. A young physics professor came to the microphone and gave a long rambling radical critique of the university, characterized chiefly by the use of a lot of clichés and jargon. At least, that's my opinion and I have probably heard more of those speeches than most people within a twenty-mile radius of anybody. He said that the university was a creature of the capitalist system (which it is, of course). He also suggested that the university's only role was to train people to serve the vested interests of society, which are not concerned with education but with manipulating the minds of the young to accept the status quo and convince them that it is in their best interest to identify with the established order. All that is somewhat usual, but he went on to suggest that they were, in fact, pawns of the economic power structure and ought to leave the university because they would learn nothing there and would probably lose their minds.

Days later, some friends suggested that the young man was a provocateur. Perhaps he was, but to show that God can use even the presence of provocateurs, the next speaker made a statement which I and hundreds of others will never forget. There was something about it which lifted me not into another world but into a state of mind whereby I could see clearly the true gracious structures of this world.

Marx Wartofsky was then chairman of the Philosophy Department, a Marxist scholar himself; he is by heritage a Jew, though I doubt whether he is very religious. That night Wartofsky entered the pulpit like a man of fire. After all, his university was being attacked, his life scorned, his integrity besmirched, but most important, the community for which Wartofsky lived, his students and colleagues, was being denied. He was mad. But there was something more than anger in Wartofsky that night. He entered the pulpit with the aspect of the heraldic lion whose mane is made of fire. I can only remember him now as huge; in reality he is a rather short stocky man. That night as he defended and proclaimed that which he loved most of all, the dialogue between human beings which seeks the truth about reality, he seemed like the embodiment of truth itself. Wartofsky suggested (though the word is somewhat academic for what he did) that the previous speaker was quite wrong. If *you* so run *your* class that the minds of students are turned off or directed into conventional, thoughtless ways, then the discussion in *my* class does not, he said. My students and my colleagues, with me, seek to struggle to understand the world, and understanding the world is one way to free the world. That, he said, is what we are properly about and that is what goes on when the university becomes community. While the academic institution may labor inside an unjust economic system, it still maintains just exactly the amount of freedom and integrity which it *takes* and struggles to maintain for itself. It is not necessary to sell out or to be manipulated; take your freedom and learn. Don't give up, take responsibility for your life and be free. It was an extraordinary speech, a speech which combined great love for people with great hope for the history of the world.

What Marx Wartofsky said was not as important as who he was or how he said it. Everyone knew that he was a man who would lay himself on the line for his students, who would work and argue for them, and who would, with great passion and honesty, argue against them if he thought it right. The passionate and committed nature of his intellectual life is a by-word among us, and that night intellect and passion seeking truth combined in as fine a defense of the freedom of the human mind in community existing against the structures of society as anyone had

ever heard. The chapel seemed to light up with his presence and around him there gathered the ancient verities —
truth, beauty, goodness, wisdom, courage, honor — as if
the Platonic ideas had taken flesh and gathered about his
head. One could almost hear the scream of the eagle of
wisdom, the roar of the courageous lion, and, in the
humility which was his in the presence of his colleagues
and students, one could discern the gentleness of the
lamb, which lies down with the lion and signifies the
fulfillment of all things.

When and if Wartofsky reads this, he will scoff at it as
irrational and sentimental, mystical claptrap. If he does,
he will be wrong.

What was necessary that night in the chapel, and what
is necessary throughout our days, is the capacity to see
through the events to the meaning behind them, to sense
in an obscure but certain manner the presence of God in
the events of the world.

> God is not so much perceived as vaguely felt and ap-
> prehended and that in a passing way and by the light of
> a sudden and momentary blaze of glory so that a great
> flame of love is enkindled within the soul. (Bernard of
> Clairvaux, Sermon on the Song of Songs, #18)

Some of us have become so accustomed to identifying
the history of our time as a time of the judgment of God
that we forget that even in our day God sends his reconciling, graceful Spirit. Many of us think that the recent history of our country, especially in the economic disarray
and social dislocations caused by the Vietnam war, provides an example of what the Scriptures mean when they

speak of the judgment of the God of history. In a number of ways, the sense of pride we had in our country is badly tattered and our feeling that the United States had a role in history which was to be a sign of justice and democracy is seriously questioned. We have indeed become the "almost chosen people." Beyond that, thousands of young men have been killed or maimed, others condemned to drug addiction; some of the finest souls have endured prison for reasons of conscience. The self-hatred with which we live has been brought on us by ourselves and by our institutions. I think that no apocalyptic in Scripture provides a more graphic example of what happens to the nation which abandons God and follows its own way than the events of American history in the last ten years.

When one of my students was asked why she liked Shakespeare's *King Lear* more than a comedic play, she answered, "I guess it's just because we know so much more of suffering than anything else, like love. So we recognize it and find it easier to understand." And that's one of what is supposed to be a generation of coddled students.

Amid the breakdown of our civilization, it is important for us to be able to point to the structures of goodness which still exist. The grace of God, which speaks to us from the voices of our imagination, speaks to that imagination out of the books we read, the plays we see, the people we listen to, and the experiences we have. Men and women used to speak of the angels of God; it doesn't matter what name we give these messengers as long as we are able to hear them and know, through them, the Word of God. I believe that Marx Wartofsky was, that night, reaching into the power and the presence of the Holy

Spirit, the presence which Gerard Manley Hopkins spoke of as brooding over the bent world "with warm breast and with ah! bright wings." The wings, I prefer to think, brushed Marx's face that night and set his tongue on fire.

When we take the world seriously, I believe that we become aware of the potentiality for creative thought and action which exists in the world as the will of God. And we learn to discern that Spirit as that which constantly aids us in the discovery of truth. In a time when many people seem hopeless, one of the signs of hope is the constant possibility, given to us through the agency of the Spirit in the world, the presence of God in our imaginations, to identify and cast down the inhuman structures of evil which are so powerful in the economic and bureaucratic systems of our time, twisting and perverting the creation toward private gain over public good and destroying the life of the Spirit in the body. We also, when we are open to the possibility of knowing God's presence in our experience, find ourselves heartened and made strong when we realize the ubiquitous nature of the human response to God's call.

We are alert to the messengers of God whenever and wherever they appear. And as we train ourselves in the expectation of the presence of God, we find that in our own personal experience God is often speaking to us. And this is not just through political or intellectual experience, but in the opportunities and problems of ordinary life. So our further discovery is that almost anything can lead us to know ourselves as persons found by God. For example, the senses can be used to bring us into the presence of God. One of those senses is feeling, even feeling pain.

It is necessary to say right away that there has been an

unfortunate tradition in Christianity which almost exalts pain and sufferings as ways to the presence of God. I can't think of anything less true. Occasionally in the midst of pain, one discerns meaning and grace, but usually such discernment is despite the pain and only through a certain kind of struggle and gift which serves to defeat the power of suffering, its despair and guilt. The crucifixion, standing as a sign of the pain of the world, does not stand alone — it has not and has never been by itself a sign of hope. Jesus' life had a double ending. The crucifixion is a sign of God's absolute involvement with us; it is the Good News that he shares our death, our loneliness, our suffering, that our finite experience is present in some way in the being of God and he is one with us in our struggle against the power of death.

But we also need the other ending of Jesus' life, the resurrection, as a sign of the ultimate structure of goodness in the universe, the hope which leads us to the discovery of hope for ourselves, hope that we might grow and might continue growing. That hope is in the hands of God, in the Body of Christ as it exists in the world among all his people, as it existed in the double ending of Jesus' life. We try to learn in every way we can to discern the evidences of God's presence among us, not only in crucifixion and judgment, which is all too obvious as we walk the city streets and look into the eyes of the men and women who walk with us, but in redeeming presence also. It is easy to see and feel the pain, to experience the crucifixion in the lives of the poor and the powerless and the godforsaken. As we do that, we ought also to see the signs of redemption, the power of God breaking through the structures of this world, creating a change in human nature, proclaiming a future, therefore, for people and for life amid the ruins of lives.

I want to tell you a story that for me is an example of the presence of God in the middle of pain and suffering. It would be easy for me to overemphasize the amount of pain, because it was my pain and I am not so brave about pain. One thing I never have to worry about is repressing pain or pretending to be brave in the face of suffering. The *via negativa* of the mystic is not, shall we say, my natural path. It does appeal to some people and they are welcome to it. Those who wish to seek suffering so that it will bring them closer to God are also welcome to it.

A blind man I know, reflecting once on his condition, said, "Blindness stinks!" His suffering is not a way to the presence of God but a constant temptation to despair. It is a deadly pit of evil which threatens to drag him down into self-pity, anger and depression. So as I discuss pain and the presence of God, I want to be careful not to affirm evil in a search for the God who always had his people's best interests at heart.

I have said enough for you to know that I am not a friend of pain. Indeed, I abhor physical pain, (I'm not so fond of psychic pain either) and I am impressed enough by my cold sweats in the dentist chair and my terror in the face of police massing for a charge so that the temptation to say that somehow these are ways for us to know the goodness of God passes me by. But pain and injustice which are defeated by the grace of God can indeed be a powerful witness to the God who acts in our lives.

A few years ago, I developed bursitis in my left shoulder. After a day or two of pain, I consulted one of Boston's best known orthopedic surgeons (What's good for the

Bruins and the Red Sox is good enough for me). He undertook to remove the calcium deposit in my shoulder through needles inserted in the top of my shoulder. Other than that it was necessary for him to use what must have been a quart of Novocain in order to deaden the pain enough for me to allow him to proceed, it was not an unbearable experience (not quite). When he had finished he stepped back and, knowing I was a clergyman, said, "Pick up your bed and walk." Being fast on my feet with a riposte in any circumstance, I responded, "You really know how to hurt a guy." Standing on the street outside the hospital I recalled those words and the irony of his being Jewish at the time of Christmas, and those recollections led to a poem:

> Gifted am I, first of us all in '72
>> with a fine collection of crystallized calcium,
>> gift packaged by my left shoulder.
> "Pick up your bed and walk," said Bierbaum
>> merrily, adding a transcendent note,
>> to a holiday arrangement of red-stained surgeon's gloves,
>> green surgical coverall and mask,
> Vestments of a solemn high mass of irrigation and cortisone.
>
> I'll have my bursitis about as long
>> as Mary and Joseph had Jesus,
>> with luck, thirty-odd years.
> I can count on it flaring up, causing trouble,
>> associating with a bad lot of companions,
>>> fighting against the conventional wisdom of bone and muscle.

Making its own peculiar life in the midst of the world of
   twist and turn.

So my bursitis is my Jesus,
      our constant companion, though somewhat uncom-
         fortable,
      it's my socket reminder, thirty years to cause trouble.
It's those things, and in one special attraction
      in a magnificent ecumenical gesture at this holiday
         season,
It, and he, are my Bierbaum.
To whom else would you turn when no one else will do?

   I needed that doctor, needed him desperately, and I was
brought to realize through the experience that I also
needed Jesus, needed his voice spiritually as much as I
needed Dr. Bierbaum's extraordinary skill, to hear Jesus'
prayer in me and for me, needed to stand in his presence,
know his gifts, understand the nature of his death and
life, know that he was now and would always be part of
my future. I'm sorry I had to have bursitis, would probably have had something of the same realization through
some other means. Some of us are just stupid enough to
need this sort of fortuitous combination of circumstance
in order to hear the voice which sounds in our imagination. It wasn't the pain, but the relief of the pain, the act of
grace through the agency of Ben Bierbaum which was the
channel of the grace of God.
   Another way in which we touch the presence of God is
in ordinary activity. I mean this in the sense that we discern the presence in doing things, that is, ordinary things,
well. The well-done task can have an integrity which

shines out of and through it and which speaks of more than either the task or the result. We think immediately of the graciousness of Shaker furniture or of the way in which Trappists go about farming or the way a sailor coils his lines and trims his sails. The way, or style, in which these people perform those tasks reveals a deep commitment to the creation itself and to the potentiality of human beings for dignity in work. Thus the style is more than surface "style," it is the grace of God working itself out in a human being. God is also present in the very ordinary things of our lives. There is a skill and a dignity and a grace in driving a car really well. Anyone who has mastered the skill of drifting or driving into a curve or who has ridden with a well-trained and practiced driver knows what I mean. One of my friends builds budgets gracefully, another comprehends a complicated bureaucratic system by a more than human act of energy, another writes with such dedication and concentration that each paragraph seems as if it was lovingly and smoothly carved from wood, such is its clarity and polish. There is a young legal aid lawyer in New York whose defense of his clients involves such skill and bravura that one must know that the wellspring of that skill is profound commitment to persons in trouble and to the possibility of justice working itself out through the law. God is not limited by our notions of what his proper role is; he reaches out to and through all people.

The same gracious quality which we sometimes think of as being reserved only for very specialized artists (ballet dancers, potters, painters, writers) can also be found in the performance of simple household tasks. I know someone who cleans an oven with verve and skill and a kind of peculiar grace which is every bit as stunning as the way he listens to a friend. And I once knew a cleaning woman who stated her faith in pungent enough terms, "If you're going to be a streetwalker, you should be the best one on the corner — so why shouldn't I do the best job I can on this messy house?" Perhaps I can best explain what I mean by telling the story of the making of the mayonnaise.

One night a number of people showed up at our house at dinner time. My wife was away, and in that situation I become the executive director pro tem of dinner. It was between semesters, one of those times when students and friends seem to gather around; they are free of worries and they take the opportunity to come by spontaneously. That's all very well if you know how to handle it and over the years we have worked out a kind of system of expanding dinner to fit the guests. The secret is simply to add more courses. You can get together a more elaborate dessert, or make a big salad or a soup or some hors d'oeuvres. The trick is to get people in on the game so you don't become angry and harassed and unable to act as welcoming as you want to be.

I decided we had better put together some first-course things and asked people to shred carrots and peel celery and put on water to hard boil eggs. Now the best thing to have with hard-boiled eggs, which otherwise are rather ordinary, is a lovely mustardy homemade mayonnaise. Young people I tell this story to often don't even know that it is possible to make your own mayonnaise, such is the low level of cuisine in our country. The students who were at the house that night were no exception. "We don't have to do that," they said, "there's plenty of mayonnaise in the refrigerator." I explained gently that for something like hard-boiled eggs, and for a special occasion when people we hadn't seen for a while were there, homemade mayonnaise was the only thing that would do; it would raise the occasion above the regular ordinary and make it into a special ordinary. (It's important not to exaggerate these things — after all, we were probably having hamburgers for the main course.) Besides, I thought, this will give some of them something to do and keep them out of my hair for a while. They allowed as how they would try it, even though they thought I was mad. I told them it would be "interesting"; and that it would taste very good.

Making mayonnaise is a fairly simple process which involves dripping oil into beaten egg yolks while continuing to beat so as to ensure the absorption of the oil by the yolks. It is not hard to do, probably one reason why commercial food processing companies make it. On the other hand, mayonnaise is not easy to make, since the oil must be dripped regularly but very slowly, and the beating must not stop through the first part of the process.

You might want to try making mayonnaise yourself. Take a couple of egg yolks at room temperature and beat them for a couple of minutes until they are sticky. Now you can beat them with anything you want, but you will want to use a wire whisk, not for any other reason but that it's more fun. Add then two or three tablespoons of vinegar or lemon juice, a little salt, and about a quarter of a teaspoon of mustard. (Mayonnaise is not snobbish, use any kind you want.) Now take a cup to a cup-and-a-half of oil and, while beating, start dripping it slowly into the egg yolks. Not so fast! Make sure you beat each drop in before you drop another and for heaven's sake, don't stop beating. Watch the oil, don't worry about the egg yolks, they're too busy to get into any trouble. A handy way to drip the oil is to let it dribble slowly down the outside of a cup or from a teaspoon. Beat more than you drip until about half a cup has been absorbed. After that, you can rest your arm and beat the oil in a little more quickly. When you've done that, and tasted it to correct the seasonings, you've got mayonnaise.

My students that night followed just exactly that procedure. They laid out a cookbook, read through the directions, gathered the materials and started the process. They were a little amused at my antique and elitist insistence on a time-consuming and laborious process done for no practical reason. But as they began to work together, and their forearms grew tired so that each in turn was forced to turn the task over to another in order to keep the beating going, they began to get more and more involved in the creation process. What they were involved in is on the surface essentially a chemical reaction. The egg yolk, under the friction of the beating, holds the oil in suspension. That is what the textbooks say, but what really happens is that two entirely dissimilar substances, oil and egg yolk, combine to form one whole new thing which resembles neither of the two. That may be a funny way to think of mayonnaise but it's true, and the best thing about it is that it gets more amazing the more you think of it. For example, I have not tasted much raw egg yolk straight, but I have tasted straight olive oil, and it's awful. Mayonnaise tastes good. Egg yolk and oil are liquid when you begin, but mayonnaise is another consistency altogether, smooth and creamy, not runny, not quivery, but gently soft and malleable.

The people who were beating the egg yolks and the oil

at my house that night were thinking about it, they were experiencing the wonder of the process, so much so that in celebration of the time when one has beaten in enough oil so that he can relax for a moment, they all shouted, with the author of the cookbook, "The crisis is over." Then, in a more leisurely way they beat in the rest of the oil. When they had finished and seasoned their creation, they were left with a lovely, glistening, smooth product, tasting neither of oil nor egg yolk but a new thing entirely its own. Something brand new lay there, dying to be poured over hard-boiled eggs and be gobbled down by hungry college students.

The young people stood back and eyed their product silently. One person said, quietly but with finality and absolute seriousness, "It's unbelievable!" And it was.

She was using that phrase in a peculiarly modern way where it means precisely that something *is* believable, though not in the way that the world believes. That is, the mayonnaise recommended itself through experience to the imagination, and was therefore believable because it had the quality of the sublime, because it was the furthest thing removed from quantification. It was believable because it was there and because they had done it, not because of data which said that it existed, even though it did exist empirically. Its real meaning, to those people in that situation, went far beyond data into another world, a world of hope and promise — such things do we describe as unbelievable even when, or perhaps more especially when, they are lying right in front of us. The experience of making the mayonnaise brought those people into another world, a world where we all can live, the world of vision and dream, a world of completeness longing for itself. "We made this, we are a part of the process of creation." That was what was unbelievable. The Spirit spoke from the ordinary, opening our eyes to the wonder of the world, and the wonder of people who can do such things together with the world, simple things, but acts of love capable of being shared. The students that night presented us all with the mayonnaise as a gift of love to everyone at the table.

We do things well, like making mayonnaise, because there is something in us which demands that we treat the creation that way. When we are open to the possibility of God speaking to us from our own experience we come closer to the things surrounding us, and find in them a presence and a potential which means that they must be taken with respect, even things like egg yolks and oil. One also does things well because it is possible to discern in the act of doing the transcendent power which makes itself known in the acts of our history. Even the lowly mayonnaise is informed by the power which exists in the atom. And, to paraphrase a parable, if that power exists in the lowly mayonnaise how much more so does it exist in the great movements of history, in the great dreams which surge up in men and women in every time, movements for creation and redemption, for the relief of suffering and the freeing of the oppressed and the exploited. "It's unbelievable." Those words point out our cynicism and our boredom, the flat and insignificant world of data and quantification. When we see the world as ours, as part of our life as creators with God, we come to understand the awe and mystery which lies inside every created thing. "It's unbelievable." For our age, that statement is, ironically enough, a proclamation of faith.

God makes himself known to us most obviously in those places which we most ignore, that is, in the ordinary processes of life. Making dinner for our friends, going to the doctor about a troublesome pain, listening to a friend speak, walking down a snowy road, God in all his power presents himself to us on those occasions, sparkling out of the creation, available to those who are open and willing to discern him there as much as he is in the relationships between persons and in the historical movements of our time. In short, God doesn't need either the earthquake, the storm, or the thunder, he comes to us in Jesus Christ to prepare in us a listening heart.

It *almost* goes without saying that it is possible for us to twist and use the creation in ways that serve only our selfishness and, under the cover of appreciating what *is* in its potential as capable of leading to the God who has found us, instead, exalt the creation itself into a god. The worship of food, in and solely for itself, is obscene. A technically perfect restaurant which has no sense of the joy of giving to people, and of creating for the purpose of providing joy, in short, a perfect cook who cooks only for the perfection of the food and not for the service of people who come to eat, leaves a tinny taste in my mouth. Making mayonnaise was a great experience, not because some people followed directions perfectly, but because they learned and grew and offered something of their learning and growing to the rest of us. Our experience, in this technologically oriented culture, is almost universally the reverse, people offer us things, not an opportunity to share in their strength and their joy.

We trust the integrity of our insight into the creation by whether the spirit we feel speaks the name of Jesus, speaks of the vulnerability of the humanity of God, suffering in and through and with his people. The One who used his body and the things around him for the reconciliation of the forsaken, the forgotten and the alone, is the same One who stands at the beginning and the end of history.

We expect to do things well. We live our life in the dangerous atmosphere of the world, in the expectation offered up to God that, in our lives and with the people with whom we live, we will meet the God of persons and things joined, to open ourselves to strengths we never thought we had, to involve ourselves in issues we thought we didn't care about, to find ourselves joined together with people we never thought we could have anything in common with. The key to putting ourselves in the place where God can find us is to do the simple ordinary things of life well, and to make sure that we do them in the company of other people, and then join together to reflect and to pray about what was done.

Doing things well, using our bodies well, recovering respect for the earth and the things of the earth are all part of a way of coming to pray. In fact, they are a way of prayer without words. We find that we have so ordered our experience and our life and our expectations that prayer as we used to think of it, saying words to God that seemed to be not connected with our lives, fades away, and we begin truly to pray. As we learn to look, to feel, and to do in the expectation of the revelation of the presence of God, we find him there dispensing his gifts with a lavish hand, expecting that we will join him in that dispensation, the distribution of what was never ours anyway to those who stand in need of it. Our prayer, that prayer which God speaks to us in creation, is in us the equitable distribution of the things of the earth.

Just as the monk or the orthodox Jew uses all the moments of his day and every movement of his life from morning to night to put himself in the way to God, so we use the ordinary events of our lives as the way to God, we use ordinary activities done well and done together with and on behalf of the people of the world, to wake us up to the presence of the one who is for us the Way. He is the Word who speaks in and through the simple, the childlike, the ordinary. To be open to God is to be open to his radical freedom, which in Jesus was used to go anywhere and be anything for the sake of his kingdom. Thus we take, as Jesus took, bread and wine and give thanks and break and distribute and thereby enter into the presence of the central reality of the universe. In those simple things, as in all simple things, we listen for the voice of our imagination which is the Word which God speaks to us.

CHAPTER FIVE

Tell Me a Story

One afternoon, Jonathan Muckdow, classes over for the day, returned to his college dormitory. On the way to his room, he stopped to check his mail. There was an envelope lying beyond the little window, so he twirled the dial and took it out. It was a bill from the university accounting office for seventy-five cents. Muckdow could not think of what it was he was being charged for; all his bills had been paid early in the school year. He went to his room and dialed the number listed to call if there were questions. A tired voice answered and told him, "No, he did not owe seventy-five cents, according to the computer print-out, he owed $11.68." The voice did not know for what he was being billed, nor, the voice suggested, would any good come from investigating. What would be good, said the voice, would be for Muckdow to stop messing around and pay his bills. Muckdow panicked and walked quickly down the street to visit the office in person. As he stood there he could look through panes of glass far across the giant office to the enclosure where the computer sat, winking its red lights at him.

He glared at it balefully and to his horror thought for a second that it glared back. At the counter, he was informed that the amount due was really $17.97, or that was what the computer said he owed, and the computer also allowed that it was high time he paid. He could have sworn he heard a snicker as, shaking his head sadly, he went out the door.

Jonathan Muckdow hurried to his room and threw himself on the bed. He was at a loss to know what to do about the bill. There is only one thing for most college students to do when confronted by a financial problem and that is what Muckdow did. He called home. His mother said that she was sure it was a mistake; she knew the term bills had been paid long ago. She would call the accounting office herself to clear it up. While she had Jonathan on the phone, she reminded him that long distance rates were much lower in the evening and postage, while high, was still lower; perhaps he could investigate the lost art of letter writing. On the other hand, it was nice to hear his voice. She hung up and Muckdow relaxed, took a book from the shelf, and contemplated studying. His nap was interrupted by a phone call from his mother. She was upset; the bill was $35.24; his library privileges were about to be cancelled. She promised to call his father and see if Dad could make any sense out of this.

Muckdow sailed off to the library to do some studying, secure in the knowledge that his parents could solve any problem between them (Muckdow was quite young). Late that night, he received another call from his mother. He could tell that she had been weeping. When he asked what was the matter, she told him that his father's secretary had called to say that Mr. Muckdow had left at 4:30 to go out for a drink and that he was muttering something about $72.67 and just when you thought you had gotten a little ahead. Muckdow calmed his mother and was relieved to hear her report that his father had just walked in, a little worse for wear but alive and well. Beyond that, there was nothing else to report and nothing apparently they could do.

You may think Muckdow was discouraged. He was. If a college man's parents fall apart in the face of a machine gone mad, what is a mere student to think? Muckdow was tired and confused and discouraged. But he did not despair.

He hesitated for only a fraction of a second, strode to the phone and began to call his friends. Soon they were sprawling everywhere in his room, gabbling, smoking, eating oranges, biting their nails. Muckdow called for silence and explained the problem. For no reason at all he owed the university money and the amount was doubling by the hour. He had called just before the meeting and a gravelly voice told him he owed $163.59 and his phone was about to be shut off. The gravelly voice giggled in the strangest way and Muckdow had the odd sensation that he was talking to the computer itself. The office surely was closed by that time.

He opened the floor for discussion. The talk went on for hours, various actions were considered, various explanations advanced. Finally, consensus was reached and students scattered purposefully across the campus. Little time remained before morning. However, there were enough of them to do what was necessary and along the way they recruited others. Everyone who heard the story was willing to give up a night's sleep for the cause. Finally, everything was done that could be done and they slouched wearily to their beds.

As the business day was about to begin and the giant university gradually came awake and shook itself, the current occupant of the presidential chair walked briskly down the steps of his house on his way to office. His mind was on the problems with which he had to deal during that day. Crucial issues had been raised, vital questions needed to be answered before the day was through. In some cases the whole intellectual world was sitting on the anxious seat waiting for an answer; in other cases, alumni were waiting for a response to their demand that he fire the football coach. A college president is an important man. Unconsciously, he noted that something had been written on the sidewalk. He hated graffiti, to him it stood for everything he abhored, authority rejected, appeals made to the emotions, proper channels of communication — all of which ran through his office — avoided. He gasped as he looked down at the sidewalk and the full enormity of the outrage struck him. Every other sidewalk block stretching from his home to his office had been painted with the slogan, "Justice for Muckdow."

He ground his teeth and cast his eyes toward what he was sure was an empty and pitiless sky. He had recently written a book in which he proved that it was empty and pitiless. Before him, a giant dormitory reared its regularity. But this morning it was not the same flat, boring, orderly vista in which he took such pleasure. For in each window of three towers of thirteen stories each, there appeared a stenciled sign, "Justice for Muckdow." He increased his pace; something was seriously wrong. When he reached his office, he found the secretaries and administrators standing huddled in small groups, for when they had uncovered their typewriters that morning, each typewriter had a half sheet of paper rolled in it and each paper read, "Justice for Muckdow." Even then, they knew only a little of the full extent of the activities of Muckdow's friends, for all over the university, as each professor stood to begin to lecture, one could hardly fail to notice that on each blackboard in each classroom in each building, the motto "Justice for Muckdow" had been chalked. In the Art History Department, each slide projector proudly projected at the beginning of each lecture the transparency, "Justice for Muckdow." And most glorious of all, in the library, the first request slip turned in by each patron that morning, instead of returning with the notation, "Out of Circulation" or "Not on Shelf" or "Removed for Binding," instead of those messages of despair, each slip proclaimed, "Justice for Muckdow." It was as if the heavens had opened and it had rained "Justice for Muckdow."

But long before any professor began his lecture, any president rose from breakfast, any typewriter was uncovered, in a brightly lit room inside other brightly lit rooms, the temperature constantly at 68°, the humidity equally carefully controlled, an enormous machine had, with a groan, turned itself on for a mere fraction of a second. Its lights glowed once, its reels spun once, its printers chattered only once. But long before anyone was awake, the machine had printed a new account for Jonathan Muckdow which read simply, "Paid in Full."

I told this story once to a group of students. They were not notably impressed by it, but some days later, it seems to me, one of those students received a bill from the bursar. It read that she owed one dollar. She knew she had paid all her bills and this was charged to her because she had paid half a bill which included odd change, and the machine had rounded off in its favor.

She thought for one horrified moment, "I am Muckdow." She gathered her friends, many of whom were also sure that the story I had told the previous Sunday had come to life, went to the registrar's office, and explained the situation. There were enough students and they made enough commotion so that the registrar himself came out to see what was going on. He took her bill, realized the awful potential, asked her to come inside with him, took from his wallet a dollar bill, paid it to the cashier, and all of them watched the computer display as the transaction was punched into the machine. When the words, "Paid in Full," appeared on the screen, together they were delighted. Triumphantly they returned to the outer office where everyone congratulated everyone else and exchanged a kind of password, "Muckdow lives."

No, there was never such a person as Jonathan Muckdow. It's a "mere" story. About the second story. Did it happen? Did it need to? I have an awful memory, maybe it did, it's likely enough. I can surmise the then university registrar, a decent man, would help out in just that way. Maybe he did, there was a rumor he heard the original story and confessed that a Muckdow could happen, or maybe it was that he swore that a Muckdow couldn't happen. Was that a rumor, or did I make it up? And now what shall we do with this thing, a Muckdow? Is a Muckdow a something, is it real, what would it look like? Does it matter?

No. At this level it doesn't matter at all. The Muckdow story is a good story, and that's enough. It says a number of things, but if we *must* give it a meaning then it is that if you think hard enough about something and get your friends together to think hard enough about something, if you work hard enough and hope hard enough, you can defeat the unspoken inhuman structures of bureacracy. It says that *your* magic is as good as any magic, as long as you remember that "there is no such thing as magic," there is just magic-skill and hard work and dreams. It's a good story, truer than if it happened, more reflective of the actuality of the depth of love in the universe and in the university than any collection of scientific data about the university. It's a good story, that's enough. It's worth telling.

One of the ways we remind ourselves of the presence of God, indeed one of the ways that we are able to communicate with other people the presence of God, is by telling stories. Telling stories is a way to reflect. In the process of making the story our own in order to communicate it, that is, to make it someone else's own, we exist in the One who holds us together with God. Stories can be the medium through which we hear and see and touch the presence of the Spirit who is God himself. We, who have eyes to see and ears to hear, are also given mouths to speak and minds to organize experience in story.

Telling stories of our experiences with God in the midst of the world is an art which has been revived recently. Before that time, it was looked down upon by most academic theologians as not quite intellectually respectable. It was, after all, just "telling stories" like primitive people, not dealing with abstract ideas, like sophisticated people. This was partially because our philosophical assumptions led us to have more confidence in abstract concepts as a means of communicating ideas about God more accurately. And in what I am about to say, I don't mean to imply that abstract ideas and philosophical categories are *not* ways to speak about God, only that concentration on them to the exclusion of other ways of speaking the unspeakable was not healthy and the tradition of storytelling is coming into its own again.

There were any number of historical reasons for the concentration on abstractions, which particularly infects the West. For example, the decision to "close" the canon of Scripture, or limit to a certain number the authoritative list of written books of the New Testament meant inevitably that writings about past events would be regarded as more authoritative and more important than writings about current events. In turn, this decision had the deleterious effect of suggesting (in a subtle way) that somehow God no longer spoke to his people through the events of their time. It seems as if all there was left to do theologically was to describe or remine past experience in philosophical terms appropriate for the age. Until recently, that was what the theological enterprise seemed to be about. Some of us found it a little boring.

This development, plus a whole complex of intellectual, social, and historical movements meant that stories were no longer told, except for the genre known as the lives of the saints, which developed its own peculiar form and its own peculiar problems of credibility. Actually what happened was that the lives of the saints were used, not as stories which stood by themselves as *story*, but as exemplars of certain ideas or virtues, and stood subordinate to those ideas, so the stories were perverted in order to make an abstract moral or dogmatic point.

At any rate, as people no longer looked to their own experience to identify the presence of God, prayer as reflection on experience was put aside and another way, or ways, of praying was developed, a method removed from history and essentially reserved for professionals. I refer to the contribution of the monastic movement. And whatever the excellent virtues of this movement, it did mean that those who were "experts" in prayer were also, by the very nature and quality of life that they had chosen, removed from the ordinary problems and joys of life, jobs, children, and so on. Above all, prayer necessarily became something removed from the ordinary. Things as ordinary as making dinner, walking down the street, talking to a friend, making love, were not seen as "proper" occasions of prayer except for removing thoughts of them from your mind as distractions to the proper subjects of prayer. So God's approaches to us through our ordinary life were defined as "distractions," as those things which bound us to the changing and mutable nature of the world. Perhaps officially they were connected to the life of God among us but in practice they were not. The dictum, "The revelation met in Jesus Christ leads us to believe that it is in the events of our history that the God of all history is to be found," was not honored.

One way of getting back to that biblical experience, to a time when men and women had a real sense of the presence of God in the ordinary events of their lives, is to tell stories. We complete the act of listening and mulling over the activity of God around us by telling stories, that is, acts rising out of prayerful meditation in the midst of the engaged life are fulfilled by writing stories and by "retailing" (re-telling, re-taleing) stories to our community — our friends, our family, ourselves. We have allowed the demythologizing movement to go far enough and now are remythologizing and developing new myths growing out of the events of our lives. Above all, we need to appreciate the category of myth itself.

Myths are stories that almost all cultures tell and which serve to preserve the history of that people in such a way as to communicate that history as special or sacred. A myth communicates the notion that what has happened to "us" is different in such a way that we are marked by it, by the way we dress, talk, and so on, and that being different gives us our own special something which no one else has. It need not mean that "we" are better; it always means that we have our own special thing, in the way that a motorcycle gang has its own "colors" (and stories which tell why the colors are chosen) and each monastic order also has its own "colors" (and stories which tell how they came to be as they are). Parenthetically, I suspect that the motorcycle gang and the monastic order probably share at least a relative credibility in their founding stories.

A myth, then, is a story which provides a context which in some way unifies life for a people. It is not an untruth, which is the way we use the word myth today, but is the truest of all stories. It is beyond empirical verification, although some myths are linked to historical events, such as the Passover story where the myth includes as an integral part of the story both history and meaning. Generally speaking the meaning of the myth is more important than the data. The language of myth is allusive and connotative, as opposed to contemporary language which is empirical and denotative. The ostensible concern of myth is an event, its real concern is the inner landscape of a person or a people. It provides a structure whereby a person or a group understands its place in the universe. That is, it speaks of the *where* the person or group came from and that visionary place *to which* it is going.

One of the most important forms of myth tells about a journey. It describes from whence a person or a people came, what their sufferings were on the road, what they learned, and how and where they "settled down." In some ways, the myth most readily available to us is the one which tells the story of our adolescence. But the great myths, such as Easter or Passover, serve to ground a whole people in time and space. They speak of "there and back again" within a cosmic scope and provide a way for young and old to understand and communicate from whence their family or group or church came, as well as the crucial events in the collective life. So most myths have always been acted out, that is, they include gestures and reenacted events which bind them into the minds of persons. One recalls the historic event by retelling and in symbolic form reenacting the primary event. In this way, we enter into the memory and the reality of the historic event and make it our own. One is overtaken (taken-over) by history.

The Muckdow story is a classic example of a myth that a group of young people might tell about their encounter with technology and bureaucracy. It tells how they were "called out" to journey and to struggle and how the experience changed them, gave them a self-consciousness and a peculiar strength. Of course, it is pure fiction (?!) and has no historical basis, so far as I know. If pressed, on the other hand, I could probably think of one.

The great myths of the peoples come with all the mythic equipment. We think immediately of the lovely question which opens a section of the Seder. Asked, significantly, by the youngest male (demonstrating at one and the same time how it has always been important for people to teach their children to ask the right question and how easy it is for exclusivist (male) mentalities to take over mythic settings) it queries, "What makes this night different from all other nights?" The answer is "because tonight we remember." And what Jews remember, of course, is the stunning tale of how God made them his people — how he made them Jews.

> My father was a wandering Aramaean. He went down into Egypt to find refuge there, few in numbers; but there he became a nation, great, mighty and strong. The Egyptians ill-treated us, they gave us no peace and inflicted harsh slavery on us. But we called on Yahweh, the God of our Fathers. Yahweh heard our voice and saw our misery, our toil and our oppression; and Yahweh brought us out of Egypt with mighty hand and outstretched arm, with great terror, and with signs and wonders. He brought us here and gave us this land, a land where milk and honey flow. (Deut. 26:5-9)

Christians remember a story which is introduced with an unasked question, "(Will you) lift up your hearts," and which continues, "In the night in which he was betrayed, he took bread. . . ."

These are both founding stories and in their case it is interesting to note that, in order to understand the latter, one must know the former. In order to know oneself as either Jew or Christian, it is necessary really only to tell these stories. Because of the second, Christians believe they are invited to participate in the first.

So one of the saddest results of the development of our scientific technological society has been the loss of the ability to tell stories, because they are not "true." The result has been to flatten our vision and to loosen our grip on our past. We have lost our story, and we hold only a sense of loss, not knowing where we are in the rush of time. We know only that we are somehow wandering through the cosmos like a lost spaceship, we belong nowhere because we have no past and no future, no place from which we came and no future to which we are going.

Americans have had a tragic experience with stories. Our nation was founded by people who thought they were building another promised land. Early statements of purpose reflect this notion of the divine urgency and promise in the task of building. Since there is no human enterprise which sooner or later doesn't go wrong, the story of the United States is the story of something going wrong in a big way. Far from being a promised land for all people, our country has been a place of slavery and suffering for large numbers of men and women. The great promise which envisioned a nation devoted to the gifts of God — liberty and justice — has been perverted into a relentless search for profit and private gain at public expense. The promise of freedom has been twisted into what is called the "free" enterprise system, freedom for the rich and the powerful to exploit the land and the people.

Meanwhile, the stories of Horatio Alger, George Washington, Abe Lincoln, Paul Bunyan, Johnny Appleseed lost their power in the presence of a technological age which has turned its back on gentleness and vision in preference to notions of growth, and winning above all.

So, for us, money is real but Moses is not real. Capital is real and real estate is real, but the lives, struggles, and victories of the poor are not real. Profit is real but the promise of sharing the future with all people is not real. The stories (myths) of America eventually collapsed from inner rot. A funny thing happens to stories and myths which are not true, that is, resemble neither the historical reality nor the reality of the heart. They refuse to bear the burden of reality and die of the rot which affects a nation which uses them falsely to promote its own goals. The Vietnam war put an end to American storytelling as it put an end finally to American innocence. We can no longer pretend to be the good guys of the world. Johnny Appleseed and Vietnam cannot exist in the same psychic space.

So we are left without stories, or at least without stories which have power to grab our hearts in healthy ways. We are the poorer for it; it could be said that spiritually we are underdeveloped precisely because we have no stories to tell about ourselves. We need a Peace Corps from some country which has preserved storytelling in order to teach us again how to build stories. But more to the point, we need to change our national life so we can tell a story we are proud to tell. We need, as has been said before, a new heart out of which a story could grow.

> God, create a clean heart in me,
> Put into me a new and constant spirit,
> do not banish me from your presence
> do not deprive me of your holy spirit.
> Be my savior again, renew my joy,
> keep my spirit steady and willing;
> and I shall teach transgressors the way to you
> and to you the sinners will return.
>
> (Psalm 51)

But it *is* possible to make a start, to begin once again to identify in small ways, in ordinary places, the way God is present, judging and redeeming us, lifting us out of ourselves into the future. I have noticed, for example, that when the alumni who were students during the tumultous times of the sixties come back to visit, they begin not to argue the ideological points which so interested them then, but to tell stories about "how it was." These stories have about as much resemblance to my memories of the period as the stories other groups of alumni tell about their college years, but it is evident that people are beginning to sort out the experience of the sixties, beginning to find its peculiar relevance to them through the medium of story. These stories which are now being told are not, on the other hand, stories about college hi-jinks, for this is a generation which had a profound effect on all our lives. Perhaps our nation is beginning to pick up the pieces of its corporate life, realizing that those who have been there and back again can never be the same, but will always be nourished by the tales which are lovingly unfolded when old friends get together. There are other things which stories can do, as in the following:

Once, some years ago, another college chaplain and I decided to celebrate Maundy Thursday by a service of foot washing. Everyone knows that that story stands in St. John's Gospel in the place which in other gospels is occupied by the story of the institution of the Lord's Supper. Since my friend is a Roman Catholic and I am an Episcopalian, we could not hold a joint Eucharist in a public way, so we decided to come at it from the other side and to celebrate Maundy Thursday the way at least one of the gospels suggests Jesus and his disciples did.

The front of the church was arranged with a semicircle of twelve chairs, towels and bowls were provided, and we waited for people to come. The thing we had forgotten to do was to recruit people to have their feet washed. So in the time-honored manner of college chaplains, we asked the first persons who came through the door to volunteer.

One of them was a student of mine. We'll call him Ned here. I asked him if he would sit in front and have his feet washed. He looked at me in horror and I knew then that I had committed another in what seems to me to be a lifelong series of faux pas. Ned had a rare disease of the nerve endings which had affected his leg and foot. He had had several operations already and his leg would be amputated the next summer. His foot was a twisted and scarred thing, barely resembling a foot. Ned said, "You mean you want *me* to sit up there with my shoe off?" I apologized for my stupidity in my usual stumbling way, probably making him feel worse, and went off berating myself for even thinking of asking him to do something which was so embarrassing.

A few minutes later, Ned came up to say, "Do you *really* want to wash my feet." Of course we did, for if we hadn't wanted to do so before, we needed to do so now.

Thus it was that in front of several hundred people, my priest colleague and I washed Ned's distorted and diseased and scarred and sacred foot. We took it in our hands, laved it with water, and patted it dry. Everyone knew what we were doing, we didn't have to explain that Ned was making an act of acceptance of his life — not acceptance of his disease, but of his life and his commitment to the future. And it was our act of acceptance too, our promise and vow to share his life in the future. We also were enacting his acceptance of us as sinners who could treat him so cruelly at one moment and, through the grace of God reaching out to us through him, share his life the next.

We understand through this story how it is that God reaches out to us through his people, in spite of ourselves, and gives us a road on which to travel.

Well, there, I've done it again, I've explained something that's obvious. But there is a time for explanation as well as a time for abstract ideas and rationalist analysis. There is, for example, a psychoanalytic explanation for the foot-washing event which is just as real and valuable as the theological explanation. Yet neither of them have the power, the authenticity, or the life-giving spirit of the story all on its own. And this spirit is what needs to be emphasized in our age. There is a time for the intuitive, the irrational, and the idea/event which comes alive, takes life into itself, becomes a life-giving Word when it is told as story, as people's experience. Whether it conforms exactly to the "facts" or not, it is part of what I spoke of earlier as the "creation of reality." Story reflects the reality of what goes on in the hearts of people better than any group of propositions or syllogisms or analytical constructs. Story has many of the aspects of poetry. However, instead of being concentrated, it is expansive. It falls all over itself in an effort, not to instruct or sum up or make clear, but to be with us, to communicate, provide a way of communion joining persons and events into one history.

Everyone knows of the respect in which all sorts of peoples have held their storyteller, the living embodiment of the tribe's imagination. Today we have only a few storytellers, almost no one is left to take the place of that man or woman who is found at the center of the ritual circle describing the wonders and glories and struggles of times past and times to be as eyes grow big as saucers all around and the elderly nod sagely — yes, this is what it is like.

When compared with the stories and myths of ancient peoples and so-called "primitive" peoples today, our stories are flat and boring; they are not invested with the broad irony and dramatic scope of the great myths of the past. Indeed, even our language becomes, it seems to me, more and more reduced and spare. We are suspicious of and embarrassed by a speaker whose language reaches beyond the ordinary, or who invests ordinary words with special meaning and resonance. Our language and our stories have come to resemble the pips and squeaks of the machines we love so much. What an irony, to be reduced to the level of our creation instead of being lifted out of ourselves into a better way of speaking, more glorious than the language we already have.

We must learn again to tell stories, and perhaps more important, learn to tell our own story, learn to savor our own history, the history of our family, the history of our beliefs, of our political group, and our own personal development. Lots of us spend thousands of dollars learning painfully and painstakingly to tell our story to counselors and psychiatrists. In many cases we are crippled because we have had no way of getting in touch with our story. So we are also out of touch with the deep feelings connected with the events of our past and our dreams for the future.

For many of us, it is necessary to wander to the world of the unconscious, the unspoken, the barely-hoped-for so that we can find what we were looking for, that part of ourselves which has been lost and without which we can never be whole.

There is a Hasidic story of a Jew of Cracow named Eizik. He is in debt and worries about it constantly. One night in a dream, a voice tells him to go to Prague where there is an enormous treasure buried under a bridge. He refuses to believe the voice, but it refuses to accept his refusal and comes again the next night, and even a third night, saying, "What, you still here, why haven't you gone to Prague?" He hadn't wanted to go to Prague because it's a difficult and dangerous journey, but after the third night, he gets himself together and goes to Prague. There he finds the bridge mentioned in the dream. Finding it is one thing, but it is not such an easy matter to discover the treasure. Eizik hangs around so much the guard becomes suspicious and hauls him before the authorities. The officer who interrogates him laughs at his story saying, "Such a stupid Jew, why, if one went wherever he was told to go in dreams, one would be traveling everywhere. Just last night I had a dream which told me that there is a great treasure hidden under a stove in the house of a Jew named Eizik in Cracow, but I am not so foolish as to travel all the way to Cracow to search among the countless Jews there to find this silly treasure." Full of joy and anticipation, Eizik hurries home and, sure enough, finds the treasure under his very own stove, pays his debts, and lives happily ever after.

One can only find the treasure which exists at home after he has taken a long and dangerous journey somewhere else. Our own stories exist inside us; it is necessary to listen to the voices of our imagination, the voice of God in us, to find the treasure which is already there. It is necessary to believe, to trust, to be willing to listen to that which God is telling us in the situations of our lives, in order to find out just what is our treasure.

As we listen to the voices which help us tell our own

story, we are aware that our story is our true prayer. The story that God speaks in our hearts as we listen, look, and feel may be that which opens the future to us, makes it clear that the direction we had been moving in haltingly was the way God was calling us to go. Our story, our very own story, that which belongs to us alone, the story which is our name, is the story God wants us to discover in his presence. He is constantly attempting to elicit it from us. So our treasure and our prayer and our story are the same thing looked at from different angles, from the point of view of the tension in us between that which we are in ourselves and that which we are active in the world. Our story is the synthesis between the thesis and antithesis in us, it is the process of our own dialectic.

In order to find our treasure we must be open to listening, ready to hear, ready to take the dangerous journey out of our commonplaces and our banality to trust in God. We are led finally to understand that our story is a gift from God, a precious treasure. And when we have heard our own story, we can then tell it, say our own name, release ourselves in the power which comes from God, send out our story, trusting that it will be returned to us enriched by the listening of many others, who may find in our story the map which allows them to start their own journey toward a presence and a treasure which will belong to them alone in the company of God and his people.

Learning our own story is one way to find out in what ways our life matters. The expectation that life will open up the future for us in such a way that we will have a story to tell, a name to give, is one way of making sure that we do have an identity.

Prayer in the sense of listening to God is a creative force leading us into the world of narrative-making and story-building in the arena of our own life. The person who can turn to his or her children or friends or students and say, "This is my story," is one who rejoices in the sharing of a treasure he has not kept under a bushel but proclaimed from the housetops.

CHAPTER SIX

Attending to God

I try to be a true attendant upon grace.
Perhaps it will come, perhaps it will not come.
Perhaps this quiet yet unquiet waiting is the
harbinger of grace, or perhaps it is grace itself.
I do not know, but that does not disturb me. In
the meantime, I have made friends with my
ignorance.

Franz Kafka

What is prayer? It is easier to say what prayer is not. Prayer is not asking God to send a parking place fast so one can do one's errands before anyone else. Prayer is not reminding God of things he might have forgotten such as bad weather, or a flu epidemic, as if he were a senile old man whose memory needed to be jogged. Nor is prayer keeping God up-to-date on fads in group relations or theological jargon, as if he were somehow absentminded or behind in his reading. Many of the prayers we make are talking about ourselves in a loud voice, usually with a great many dependent clauses.

Prayer does not begin with talking to God at all, prayer begins and ends with listening to God. The way we often go about praying would lead one to think that God is dead or at the very least, comatose. We make and hear prayers that seem to have no real expectation of his action. We yell at him things we think he ought to know, but meanwhile we have things under control. Real prayer trusts that God is faithful to his promise, that he is involved in strange and unexpected ways in history, that he is the living God.

If being aware of what is going on is a part-time occupation for us, it is a full-time occupation for him. We know that God is not limited in the way we covertly try to limit him, that is, to that which is inside our world view. Prayer is the simple act of trust that God is concerned about us and wishes us truly to be persons living under his rule, and that he has high hopes for us. We listen carefully to

127

the voice of our imagination for what it is that God is trying to draw out of us.

> One kind of person thinks and imagines that when he prays, the important thing, the thing he must concentrate upon, is that God should hear what he is praying for. And yet in the true, eternal sense, it is just the reverse; the true relationship in prayer is not when God hears what is prayed for, but when the person praying continues to pray until he is the one who hears, who knows what God wills. This kind of person, therefore, uses many words, and therefore, makes demands in his prayer, the true man of prayer only *attends*. (S. Kierkegaard, *Journals*, p. 97)

Prayer is confronting the problems and decisions of our life, not as if they are inevitable or already decided in advance, but as issues to be spread out before God as we learn to expect him to elicit judgments and decisions in accordance with his purpose. So prayer is expecting that our human nature can be changed. That is, prayer involves the assumption that when we open ourselves to God in the context of our lives, our lives will change and our human nature will move in the direction of greater strength and unity with the people around us and greater unity with the people of the world, especially the poor. Prayer, in that sense, is making sure — by submitting our decisions to God and listening for his decision and his Word — that we do not build our happiness on the misery of others.

One of the reasons why so many of us are bored and

depressed, indeed, one of the reasons why we seek sensation, is that we do not pray, do not have hope for change
in our lives, do not think that the systems in which we are
caught can be changed. The hope for change, for things to
be better, is part and parcel of what is meant by prayer.
Prayer intrinsically involves political judgment, and
decision-making politics is part of what it is all about. The
spiritual and political conditions of our lives cannot be
separated. The power of death can run from political
hopelessness to spiritual despair and vice versa.

So one of the reasons why the manipulators of the world
and their servants *use* prayer and false spirituality to rein-
force the idea that human beings are weak and cannot,
indeed, ought not be strong and active in the world is
because prayer is such a powerful tool for gaining strength
and purpose. What Louis Evely calls pagan prayer —
prayer which treats God as an idol, as one to whom we
turn in an attempt to manipulate him into giving us what
he has already given us — is used to communicate a false
dependence on God suggesting there is something more
important than the struggle to redeem the world in its
fullness. The sort of prayer which always seems to involve
considerable instruction of God in what he ought to do
implies that we are helpless before God (we are) and the
notion that he is best pleased when we are helpless,
period. Depression and resignation from the human
struggle is a political weapon wielded by those who wish
to preserve the status quo. Their weapon involves defining prayer in such a way as to leave out the possibility that
God might raise us up in wrath to "pull down the princes
from the thrones and exalt the lowly, to fill the hungry
with good things and to send the rich empty away." Real

prayer waits for that possibility and assumes that the strength to do that in due time will be provided as we ask for it and prepare ourselves for it. Many of us have been taught to be more humble than God wants us to be. Everything we know about him from Jesus Christ leads us to think that God wants us most of all to be real people, full of authentic ego, knowing our names, secure in our identity as his children.

In prayer, we admit where our strength ends and where we are weak, but in prayer we also touch the source of strength and strive to change the parts of our weakness that are changeable. Prayerful people often find that cherished resentments and rigidities are precisely the places where God is asking us to change, expecting us to change, and giving us the ability to change. In prayer we are never more fully aware of ourselves as strong and also never more fully aware that our strength is not enough. When we have come to the limits of our strength, when we have done everything we could do, that is the time to pray to be given more strength, more insight, more possibilities, more options for the future. Prayer does not excuse us from action, or often counsel us not to act; most often it propels us into action. I think that it is likely not to be prayer if it does not do that.

Though it is anthropomorphic and foolish to push the theological metaphor of parenthood too far, if we reflect on the analogy between God and human parents we discover a startling insight. Parents do not raise their children to grow up and love them. That is not the purpose of parenthood. Children are raised to grow up to be able to love others and so to pass on the love of parents. So it is reasonable to suggest that God does not love us in order that we will grow up to spend our time loving and praising him, but so we will communicate his love and righteousness to his people, so they in turn can reach out to others. I do not believe we can talk about prayer for its own sake, but only for the sake of the world for which Christ came and gave his life.

There is so much sloppy talk and writing about prayer, so many sentimental things written about it, that many strong people would rather not have anything to do with it. Prayer, as it is so often presented, is an insult to our humanity. One would almost think that there was a conspiracy to keep people who are strong and happy and put-together from thinking that they could ever pray at all. The Church sometimes seems to say, "This is not for the likes of unspiritual you." Certain false theologians and political theologians seek to convince us of our weakness and offer nothing to strengthen us for struggle against the powers and principalities of the world. They seek to keep men and women *dependent* on a false god, a god of consolation and comfort. It helps when we come to prayer to remember that when we begin to speak about supernatural things, we should include in our thinking vast doses of common sense. Usually our inner savvy about what is consistent with what we know of God will save us from sentimentality.

In one of his novels, J. D. Salinger suggests that sentimentality is giving something more emotion than God does. When one looks into Scripture we find little sentimentality. Jesus has feelings, is angry, is reported to have wept, but no one could say that he is sentimental. The literary style most used in Scripture and in the writings of many of the saints seems to be *irony*, and the miracles and heavenly events pictured in the Bible are narrated dryly with a great sense of reserve. Gentle irony is perhaps the most appropriate mode of religious discourse. When we come to pray, we realize that our experience, our dreams, our visions are small and mean when compared to the expectations of God for the world. We discover in being known by God his great expectations — his intent to move us into the radical and overwhelming freedom of Jesus Christ.

It is also helpful to keep in mind the startling idea that God really intended the creation of the world and the redemption of the world. That is, it is through human history that he reveals himself most fully, and it is in our history personally and corporately that he still reveals his story and his body. God is committed to the world by acts and words that go far beyond any commitment we might make to him. Particularly, it is in and through a particular people that he reveals his presence, that is, whether we like it or not, God needs and intends to reveal himself in us. Jesus has no body left now except us; he has no arms, no legs, and no mouth except ours and in him God commits himself to us now and forever. It is in the face of those around us that we see Christ and through him we are enabled to see the glory of God.

But indeed, we exist solely for this, to be the place he has chosen for His presence, His manifestation in the world, His epiphany . . . if we once began to recognize humbly but truly, the real value of our own self, we would see that this value was the sign of God in our being. Fortunately, the love of our fellow man is given us as the way of realizing this . . . It is the love of my lover, my brother or my child that sees God in me, makes God credible to myself in me. And it is my love for my lover, my child, my brother, that enables me to show God to him or her in himself and herself. Love is the epiphany of God in our poverty. (Thomas Merton, "As Man to Man," *Cistercian Studies* 4:93-94, 1969.)

The first time I met the man who became a kind of spiritual counselor or director for me, I did so not knowing what to expect and rather feared, even expected, to be sent off, in the fashion of the desert fathers, to make the flight of the alone to the alone, to seek spiritual experience beyond time and space. I was amazed and relieved to hear him say that if I ever found myself lifted out of myself, away from my experience and my body, that I should stop whatever it was that I was doing immediately. It would be wrong. It was, in any case, not the sort of thing we were going to be after, which turned out to be reflection on the incidents and history of my life in the presence of God. That direction, to be down-to-earth, was the only direct order he ever gave me. And I found, as I walked and prayed and listened for the voice from the imagination, that if I peopled my thoughts with the faces and images of the people around me, if as I walked, I looked not to the sky or across the ocean but at the lives being lived, that I could avoid the temptation to seek consolation in religion, and instead seek the strength in me through God.

That is not to say that traditional methods and prayer and ways of going about being touched by God are not authentic for many of the people doing them. Different people flow to different methods and different kinds of prayer. There are individuals who will never be satisfied until they are in absolute silence and making the ancient journey alone into the presence of the God who meets them beyond word and experience. For most of us, however, embracing that kind of spirituality would mean repudiation of the lives we have freely chosen, in God, to live; it would mean repudiation of our families, our work, our political struggle, and the bodies under whose burden we do not groan, but in whose splendid workings we rejoice. For most of us who are not called to monastic life, the purpose for us in Jesus Christ is to be found in a struggle in and through the world to which God committed himself forever and ever in Jesus.

God did this because he wanted to. It was not something he was forced into, or a second alternative, as lesser evil. He never acquiesced in the break brought about by Adam's decision. He came to us and loves us because he wants to, it is his will. Nothing we can do will get him to change his mind. It is his nature, so far as we know it, to be for us, freeing, loving, struggling, and dreaming in us.

And that is what is real. The ancient world argued constantly about what is real. For the Greeks, ideas of truth, beauty, and goodness were more real than any other thing (except perhaps ideas of unity and duality). In their culture with its enormous changes in fortune (as in Homer or Euripedes, for example), its concept of all-or-nothing conflict, the notion that what was real is unchanging, dispassionate, and eternal was freeing. It gave men some breathing space. It enabled them to rise out of the senseless cruelty of battle, the never-ending flux and threat of creation, and out of the fear of dying forever. The Jews believed, on the other hand, in a God who was totally committed to the creation, not as fragmentary or cyclic reality, nor as an end in itself, but as the setting for freedom and justice and loving-kindness shared among all people. In the Old Testament, there are the seeds of a notion of God who is identified with the life of his people in such a way that he shares that life himself.

At least the Greeks and the Jews wondered about reality; our "sophisticated" modern world accepts the natural world, the flux, the data, as the *sole* reality. Tragically, it believes against its own inclination it is going nowhere. The world to which too many of us belong believes that our life has no significance. On the contrary those of us who worship Yahweh, the Lord of history, the only God who is God, are stuck with believing that we find significance and life in the world through the reality of God's loving rule. God has already given us everything, including the most precious things — the ability to make decisions and use our freedom. While the proper use of freedom remains a stumbling block, Christians trust God to renew the possibility of obedience and abundant life continually. We ask him to accept what he gives us, we make ourselves open to his love, ready to be changed into people who do his will not because it is an "ought" but because it grows out of the needs of our hearts. In short, we seek to love him in the way he loves us, freely and without reservation. Through the Spirit in us we seek his gift of life offered for all people, that is what he chooses to give us as his prayer to us.

One of the best stories in the fourth Gospel tells of the disciples sitting around, depressed and bored, after the crucifixion. Peter, as ever energetic and irrepressible, leaps up. "Let's go fishing." They troop off to the boat and set out to work out the soreness from their hearts. The best cure for sadness is to learn something or to do something and there is always something to be learned from the water, the boat, and the fish. Suddenly they see a fire on the shore about the length of a football field away. Since they're catching nothing anyway and they're curious, they make their way toward it. They see a figure, someone they don't recognize (people never recognize Jesus in his post-resurrection appearance, it is always something about what he does, or the peculiar setting, that brings them to him). The person on the shore suggests that they "throw 'er o'er stabb'rd" and when they do, the net is filled with fish. There is something about this event which brings them to a partial realization of who it is. When they move in closer they can tell that it is Jesus. Peter jumps in the water to swim to him. (Curiously enough, he wraps his cloak about him; perhaps he liked to swim in his clothes, perhaps he was modest!) When the disciples get to the shore, they find he has cooked a breakfast of broiled fish and bread. He is no desert ascetic: they share a fisherman's breakfast. Reading about scriptural moments like this, I always recall Pope John visiting with the Vatican gardeners and, finding they had been under orders to "disappear" when he walked in the garden, orders bottles of wine brought in. Toasting them he says, "This is dry work." Surely there was a skin of wine to share there on the shore in the morning coolness.

After breakfast, the Scripture records that Jesus pulls Peter aside. Three times he asks if Peter loves him. What can Peter say? Despite the past, despite the betrayals, despite the easily made promises of the past, he says, "Of course, you know I do." And Jesus tells him, each time,

"Then feed my sheep . . . Feed my Lambs . . . Feed my Sheep."

The love which we have for God in Christ, and the love he has for us is part of the same movement of love toward the world and is also part of a great stream of love realized only when it is carried to the people around us. The words of Jesus are arranged into separate statements, "Do you love me? . . . feed my Sheep." But they exist here and in our experience as a unity inside the tension in which God exists and through which he reaches out to us. The movement toward God in Jesus through the Spirit is "usward," and also the movement through us as Body of Christ in the Spirit to everyone who stands in need of us is the same power of God. We wait prayerfully to hear the voice of God directing us to the other, reaching out to the people around us and building us into a society in which people are treated and loved as God treats and loves his people, compassionately and with great hope for their future. God reaches out to us through others, God reaches out to others through us, giving us his strength which enables us to share his vulnerability.

Prayer of that sort does not come easily. It requires honesty and willingness to hear what one does not want to hear. Indeed, it is just when prayer is hardest that one discovers the importance of going on. It is then that one discovers what it is in him that is blocking the Word of God. This waiting and wanting, knowing that one must turn and ask, must allow the Lord who waits and knocks to come, is also prayer. I remember spending a restless Sunday wandering around the house, doing all the little jobs that didn't particularly need doing, pinching back some plants, rearranging some books, feeling more and more miserable, wondering all the while about a decision I had to make, and finally walking into the study to open the Bible to read quietly and to wait, to understand that the restlessness was in itself a Word from God, calling me to myself, calling me to wait and to decide.

In waiting, we understand the radical nature of our freedom with God. He never forces us, he draws us with bands of love. That love is *our* freedom and *his* openness. But when we finally are able to hear the Lord speaking through the voice of our imagination, the moment is clear. The Word is clear and true.

Still, given our tendency to rationalization and corruption, the Word must be tested. Scripture gives innumerable examples of men and women testing the Spirit, seeking guidance as to whether a Word is from the Lord or from somewhere else. The story about the annunciation of Mary demonstrates the testing of the Word. First, after she had heard the message of the angel, Scripture records that she took time by herself to think things through. She did not rush out in the first flush of excitement, but waited to calm down and consider before she made any decisions. Then, so far as we know, she consulted Scripture. At least, we infer this from the report of the angelic announcement and her reported response in which she quotes Scripture freely. At least the gospeler felt entitled to put these words in her mouth as a part of what must have been felt to be a believable account of the event. And then she went to talk to her friend, Elizabeth, to consult someone else in the community. So Mary is reported to have 1) listened and pondered what she felt was a message to her; 2) set it alongside Scripture and tradition to see if this Word was consistent with the experience of the past; 3) consulted members of her community.

It is OK to pray by oneself, indeed, it is necessary much of the time. But decision making on the basis of prayer must be as much a communal event as it is a personal event. This is part of the function of the gathering in God of the community of the faithful. And while Jesus went off by himself to pray, we also know that he engaged in conversation with his friends when he raised issues of what to do and where to go. (We seem mostly to have stories about his ultimate decision, but occasionally we catch glimpses of the process.) Jesus was intimately conversant with the scriptural traditions, and seems also to have tested his decisions against those traditions, even when the result was a decision to break with the tradition. We might even say that it was especially those cases in which the tradition was consulted.

So, in Kierkegaard's words, we *attend*. We *attend* the presence of God speaking around us, we *attend* to the tradition, we *attend* to our friends who often know us well enough to know when we are fooling ourselves. We have to learn to set them free in order to empower them to tell us those things. Those of us who are parents know how amazing it can be when we find time really to talk seriously with our children, to attend to them. On a long trip when ordinarily time would be spent listening to those awful songs they listen to on the radio, or chatting idly about things along the roadside, when I ask some important question about our life or the life of the family, I am often stunned to discover how thoughtful and observant they have been and how carefully and loving they can call a parent to account. So when we stop telling a son or daughter what to do and listen to what it is they see when they consider the family situation, when we attend to them, we are almost always sure to learn something and to marvel at them. In the midst of a discussion I once suggested my daughter was "too critical." "I wonder," she said dryly, turning to look at me, "where I got that trait anyway?"

We *attend* to God as he raises questions, and points us to decisions. We *attend* on him, we do not wait for quiet or for absolute confidence. If we were to wait for quiet, we would wait for another Eden, and that is not the deal. We speak to God of what is happening to us, out of the events and concerns of our life, and we speak to the God who listens and who speaks and who acts in history. And we learn to expect surprises as he challenges us to do more than we think we can do and gives us the opening and the peace and strength to do it. In that listening for the prayer of God, we realize that we have been known far more than we know, and that the one who knows us is acting through us.

> I try to be a true attendant upon grace. Perhaps it will come, perhaps it will not come. Perhaps this quiet, yet unquiet waiting is the harbinger of grace, or perhaps it is grace itself. I do not know, but that does not disturb me. In the meantime, I have made friends with my innocence. (Franz Kafka, *Conversations with Kafka*, G. Janovich)

CHAPTER | SEVEN

Walking with Feet

*But since the reality of all Christian meditation
depends on (the recognition of our true self)
our attempt to meditate without it is in fact
self-contradictory. It is like trying to walk
without feet.*

Thomas Merton, *Contemplative Prayer*, **pp. 70-71**

I began to pray on Huron Avenue in Cambridge, Massachusetts. That looks funny in black and white. You should have been there; it was even funnier. In fact, it started out as a joke, as so many things do with me. That is one reason why I know that what I heard that day was really something of a Word, because funny things have always come into my head, and always have come into the heads of everyone in my family. Perhaps it's because our roots are set in a bunch of French Huguenots whom history condemned to live for several hundred years in Northern Ireland cheek by dyspeptic jowl with a nasty crowd of dour Scots Presbyterians. That, and the fact that the other side of the family fought the good fight to unionize the coal mines of Northern England blessed by a touch of Welsh madness, is maybe why I have such a strong sense of the absurd. I think sometimes that laughter would have been completely lost to Ulster if my ancestors hadn't gaily told stories and joked around amid the hatred and the grit. Even now, amidst all the bloody horror of that place, I'll bet a Ferris is getting and giving a laugh somewhere, probably wondering in his or her heart why everyone else is so earnestly serious.

So when I finally learned to listen for God speaking in the events of my life — which is what prayer must be for me — what would be more natural and real and true than that it would come in the middle of a joke. It was so somehow *right* — the Lord doesn't care how he reaches us . . . he finds us where we truly are, joins us in our jokes in

143

order to speak to us, just exactly because our jokes are so much who we are.

Anyway, it happened like this. I decided, somewhat skeptically, to learn to pray, partially for all the reasons which have been set down heretofore. Partially, of course, I really didn't *decide* this — as when you "sit down and decide" — I mean, I resolved to see if the presence of God ought to be realized by me more clearly, more personally. It has always seemed to me that the presence of God in history, in my history, as American, Episcopalian, male, white, etc., is obvious, and I thought and still think that this presence in our commonality is just as important as presence in individuality.

It occurred to me over the last few years that for all the reasons to which I alluded earlier, reasons of personal authenticity, that I should be more what I purport to be, that I should allow myself to be investigated radically by the presence of God — and at the very least, submit myself to one of the traditional disciplines to be open to whatever it was that God wanted to say to me, even if it was "nothing."

I had to do that in terms of a particular discipline or else I wouldn't do it at all. That's the way it is with me. I decided to let myself be manipulated within a structured situation by people who were expert at what they were doing, and all the while I would, of course, be myself.

I decided to go to the Jesuits. The nasty old Jesuits. And for a number of reasons. First, they were across the river in Cambridge, that is, handy. (Do Jesuits like being described as handy?) I had heard good things about the center, its rigor, sense of purpose, commitment. I had also heard bad things about it, one-factor analysis, rigid mold into which each retreatant must fit. All that ambiguity was reassuring because it meant that the Jesuits were serious about that which they were up to. They weren't bland, weren't doing the same old things for the same old reasons.

I was also sure that I could easily say to hell with it, and there would be a lot of people around who would say "terrific." Since there was support on both sides of the opinions about the Center for Religious Development, I entered into my work with them with more freedom than I would have if there had been some unanimity.

I also went to the Jesuits because I had been doing some reading in the area of spirituality, trying to get a feel for various traditions, and had already decided that the major tradition other than the one which the Jesuits embodied, a more withdrawn, monastic (*via negativa*) tradition was not for me. It simply doesn't fit the life I have chosen to lead and I have serious doubts whether it fits the life of anyone who lives outside an enclosed community.

The last reason why I wanted to work with the Jesuits was that they were doing something old, the Spiritual Exercises of Ignatius of Loyola, their founder. That may sound a little strange, for after all, parts of this book may seem to be rather "new." I guess I would have to say that while I constitutionally like new "things," I don't necessarily like new "ideas," having been betrayed by one or two in the past.

So, having been a college chaplain through the sixties, the Beatles and the New Left and all that, I thought I could do worse than pick up on something old, so long as I did it as myself, as a modern man. Old ideas, modern selves, new content, old forms, might be the motto. The Jesuits

had renewed the Spiritual Exercises of Ignatius Loyola —
they were doing old things in a new way.

Working through the Exercises with a Jesuit sounded
scary and I find a lot of people think that it *is* scary.
They're right — it is. Not because, I suppose, of what one
might be asked to do. One can always do things in a
half-baked way, a way that doesn't affect you seriously,
the way I had done so many things in my life. But because
of the way the Center set things up, I hoped to be able to
enter into the experience of prayer in a disciplined, serious way.

I found the Jesuits to be struggling like everyone else,
and rather expect that their recovery of the Exercises had
been as much an act of desperation as anything else. The
rumor was that they were trying to come up with something special, which would be their contribution to the
renewal of the Church, and the only thing on which they
could agree was Ignatius. (If you know the Jesuits, you get
the impression that there is possibly only one fairly sac-
rosanct thing left for them, and that's Ignatius.) Who
would argue against Ignatius? Many Jesuits could and did,
not against so much as with and the result was a renewal
of the Exercises shot through with modern psychological
insights and an offer by the New England Jesuits to lead
any person through them who wanted to be led. I wasn't
really sure how far I wanted to go, but I was sure that I
wanted to spend my time opening myself to the presence
of God with someone and something serious and tough.
One thing you can say about Ignatius and the Jesuits,
they're serious.

The Jesuit with whom I was supposed to work appeared
soon after I made arrangements with the Center. I had
expected, at the very least, the aquiline features, the face

hidden in the shadow, the rich black cassock of Stephen Daedalus' director — page 144 of my copy of *Portrait of the Artist*. *My* spiritual director wore jeans, smoked more cigarettes than I did, came from much the same background — Irish but not Ulster — and was even *shorter* than I am. Clever people these Jesuits, diabolically clever. It seemed to me when I saw him that the Hound of Heaven must be on my trail, for it was clear that there would be no easy outs for me now. I don't mean to say that he and I were exactly the same; I found him a little too psychologically oriented, a little "liberal" in theology, perhaps a little too oriented to feelings, not enough to ideas, but very sensitive to who I am and why I'm that way, and hard as nails about not letting me off the hook. It could have been chummy (we're-all-in-the-ministerial-club-together), and it was chummy — but not when we got to the nitty-gritty of prayer.

We found that the rich mixture of our backgrounds and attitudes helped us move along, we weren't "alike" at all. Some things which came naturally easy to him, bursts of praise or thanksgiving, came hard to me, husked about as I am by a well-learned WASPy shell, while on the other hand, something such as preaching, which connoted to him a dry and lifeless form of communication, is for me an exciting and challenging opportunity.

So these two unlikely sorts sat down to grapple with a yet less likely sort: Ignatius of Loyola, Spanish-soldier/saint, leader of the Counter-Reformation. After all, there is irony enough for anyone in the situation of an Anglican priest sitting down to work through exercises which were used at least in part to train men to go to England to undermine the English Reformation.

I ended up, after nine months, going through a couple

of weeks of the Exercises. (They are organized in four weekly series of meditation.) That pattern of working through the long retreat, as it is called, follows a suggestion of Ignatius that people who must carry on their lives while making the Exercises should spread the experience out over a longer time than the basic thirty-day period. In any case, we didn't stick with the rigid pattern as conceived in the sixteenth century, nor with some of the attitudes contained in the Exercises as Ignatius wrote them, but we did make a good run at it.

That is why I found myself on Huron Avenue in Cambridge in the middle of a joke, beginning to pray, that is, beginning to listen to God. Who was saying to me through my imagination the most perfectly simple obvious things that I would never have said to myself in a thousand years. And that was that he had blessed me with a million things, with gifts and talents and ideas and wife and children and friends. And in those gifts and those experiences was his love for me. Just that.

> fine as oil on the head,
>   running down the beard
> running down Aaron's beard
>   to the collar of his robes;
>
> copious as a Hermon dew
>   falling on the heights of Zion,
> where Yahweh confers his blessing,
>   . . . .
>
> (Psalm 133)

That is what it was like on Huron Avenue in Cambridge

and many other times since. Not in a happy, count-your-blessings way — God has been good to us, yum yum — but just as a matter of what is real to me. God has been good to me, and I never realized in what a straightforward way until that day. And I thought *I* was a joker.

I am a long way ahead of myself. You would be interested to know how I got to that street corner and what the joke was. On the surface that is the easiest question of all to answer. I was walking, meditating, and the joke was that I was praying. How's that? Satisfied? I thought not. Let me spin it out.

Frank had suggested that I meditate on Isaiah 49:1-6. That rather formidable word, "meditate," can be taken in all sorts of ways, (and in one transcendental case can be taken commercially) and I suppose I ought to say just what it is that I mean.

I don't know exactly what it is that I mean. But let's say that meditate for us will mean "think about seriously," and we will understand it as implying that when one meditates or thinks seriously he is opening himself to the potential truth reality will reveal to him or her. Probably it's a good idea even to avoid the use of the word meditate altogether, since it has come to mean something deliberately and thoughtfully removed from the world in which the meditator lives. According then to the conventional religious way of thinking, if meditation did have something to do with the world of history and personal experience, it meant only that it was a subject of meditation as an example of despair and sin, rejected out of hand by God, and not a place of good and evil loved by God in spite of itself, filled with the Spirit, and struggling against the greatest of odds to come alive.

However, when I speak of meditating, I want to think seriously about the world in just those latter terms, and to let the mind go as it considers the self and the experiences of the self, and to watch where the mind goes and ask, "What is God saying to me in this?" I would not worry if there was not some sort of "religious" experience or if God didn't "say anything" at all, but think calmly why it might be that he wasn't "saying anything" and to wonder if he was "saying something" in not "saying anything."

I'll write out the passage and invite you, as a favor to me, to read it over a few times, see what words stick in your mind, let your mind come back to them, allow your imagination to play around with them, and see if God is "saying anything" to you. Then I will tell you about what he said to me one day, I think.

Yahweh called me before I was born,
from my mother's womb he pronounced my name.

He made my mouth a sharp sword,
and hid me in the shadow of his hand.
He made me into a sharpened arrow,
and concealed me in his quiver.

He said to me, "You are my servant (Israel)
in whom I shall be glorified";
while I was thinking, "I have toiled in vain,
I have exhausted myself for nothing";

and all the while my cause was with Yahweh,
my reward with my God,
I was honored in the eyes of Yahweh,
my God was my strength.

And now Yahweh has spoken,
he who formed me in the womb to be his servant,
to bring Jacob back to him,
to gather Israel to him;

"It is not enough for you to be my servant,
to restore the tribes of Jacob and bring back the survivors of Israel;
I will make you the light of the nations
so that my salvation may reach to the ends of the
earth."

(Isaiah 49:1-6)

I should say that I know, and I know that you know, that
this is part of one of the "servant songs" of Isaiah. Its
reference is corporate, not individual, that it is an interesting passage, critically speaking, that it contains all sorts of
phrases that tick off in us feelings and thoughts that some
people might think are more significant psychoanalyti-
cally than theologically. The series of words — mother,
womb, sword, shadow, hand, sharp, arrow, quiver — is
enough to keep your neighborhood psychiatrist going for
a month or two. And if the naturally sexual images that
those words must be associated with in our post-Freudian
culture come to your mind, then let them, but don't, at
least for the purposes of thinking through this with me,
don't hang around with them more than you want to. If
they want to linger, linger with them and note what
comes; if they want to go, let them go, try not to get
involved with them because you think you ought to —
not, as the man says, on my time. In short, don't pick at
them, use them as springboards to move on and through
and behind the biblical text to the Word which it speaks to

you in its fullness. What does *it* mean to to you, what is being said to *you*, not either to ancient Israel or to someone who is investigating his or her sexuality.

My response to this passage was much the same as yours probably is. I dived into the obvious symbolism and got hit between the eyes with a few memories and thoughts I would rather not have had, family things, really. Whatever that meant, it became clear that something was going on in my head, that doors had opened somewhere and all sorts of things were coming out. You must remember that I had never done much of this before. Like many of you, I had not spent time in therapy or analysis and had always been on retreats where one beat his head against the brick wall of "a way to pray." I had never really let God have *his* way with me, which is what you are doing when you hold the Word in your mind and simply say — or not *say* — "Lord, is there something you want to say to me?" or simply stop to let go, open the door. "I am listening, Lord, speak, what are you saying about my life — I have finally decided to let you find me."

In the middle of Huron Avenue in Cambridge, Mass. found.

Larry Rouillard, a campus ministry colleague, stopped me as I started out of the library where I was doing research and asked where I was going. I said, rather diffidently, that I was on retreat and was off to meditate for my daily hour. I was going to walk out Huron Avenue and see what happened.

"Well, be careful," he cautioned, "if you have a spiritual experience in the middle of Huron Avenue it would be dangerous, you could get hit by some Boston driver." Ha, Ha, we both said, wouldn't that be ironic. (Irony is all the rage in campus ministry these days.)

I walked off and let the passage rumble its way through my mind, as perhaps you are doing. The days before I had been rather amazed by the memories and thoughts that came crowding in, but I had tried simply to hold them there and say, "What do you make of this, Lord, what are you saying to me." I thought of my parents, my wife and children, my old friends, my high school days, memories so strong you could taste and smell them. Some of them were exceedingly bitter.

I thought I knew what I was supposed to "get." Clever people, these Jesuits, isn't it typical of them to choose something with all those sexual and theological associations? "I have toiled in vain, I have exhausted myself for nothing." That's what every American thinks, we have all worked so hard and for what. We have striven and delved and consumed and "what's it all for." Really, Frank, I thought, what a transparent technique and what an unremarkable idea. I should say that through the rest of the year, I would say to Frank that what he was asking me to mull over contained not very remarkable ideas, couldn't he think of something more profound rather than the same thing that everyone has been saying for the past ten years (or the past two thousand years). He would always ask me to give God a chance to speak to *me* (not the religious sociologists) for in this sort of prayer it isn't the *concept* that counts, it's how God vivifies that concept through your life. Even though I knew that to be true, I thought it a little obvious to lead *me* down the male-menopause American-myth road. I could give the answers to these propositions with my theological and political hands tied behind my back.

But it wasn't obvious, or rather, that isn't what was obvious about it. What was suddenly obvious to me at that moment in the middle of Huron Avenue was that I hadn't toiled in vain, nor had I exhausted myself for nothing, but in fact I had had a marvelous life, that in some ways I had been given remarkable gifts, had been surrounded by vast numbers of people who had cared for me and loved me far beyond my deserving and beyond whatever work I had done. The two lines "I have toiled in vain, I have exhausted myself for nothing" were not exactly true for me, but the whole passage was true in just the way it was written, not in the way the contemporary theological morality would have it, as a critique of society (that generally true notion was not true for me in the same way) but in the way it appeared to me in my life. For whether God had done any of the other things in me, he had made me his servant, he had given me his strength in and through the people to whom I was supposed to minister. And all the while I thought I had done it by myself. It hadn't been enough for him to make me his servant, he intended to reach out through me to the people around me, and he had done so.

I didn't get hit by a car, because a real spiritual experience, at least for me, is not like that. In fact, it makes you more aware of the cars, gives you light feet, and draws you to look in the eye of every driver who comes by. (In any case, that is the only way to survive in Boston.) Such an experience can be described less as a flame of fire or some other conventional mystical metaphor but more as a sensation of being in a room, realizing the reason why you are alone is because you have not opened the door, then opening the door and, when you turn from doing so, finding out that the room has been full all along. Thus, because of what you have understood, *known* by the realization of your *being known,* your future opens up and becomes different. That is the best way I can put it . . . in terms of consequences.

Isaiah was right. I hadn't exhausted myself in vain, if I had exhausted myself at all. I had none of that sense of desolation at that time. Down deep, I realized my belonging to an enormous community, some believing, some not believing, but persons who regarded me as me and as part of their life and who had allowed me to march with them into the future which was ours together insofar as it was God's.

The discovery was that this Scripture was true for me in ways that are inexpressible. It may seem obvious to other people, but the truth of that selection as truth-in-experience, truth for me, reality, was made apparent that day on Huron Avenue. It came as part of a joke and as part of a way of being critical, seeming to disagree with the Scripture, in short, as part of the way things happen to me as the particular peculiar person I am.

I found throughout the period of the retreat — and this is still true as I pray — that God would speak to me in the voice of my imagination at the most absurd times and places — showing in the strangest and most intimate way possible that I was known. I suppose there are people who hear the Word in orderly, logical ways. I hear the Word at the moment I least expect it, and it always seems to contradict what I had assumed to be true and yet the Word (insofar as one can pin down the unpindownable) speaks in ways that are self-authenticating — need no proof. One knows in being known.

All through the fall and winter of that year, I continued to pray under the guidance of Frank, and the Lord continued to speak, not promiscuously or literally but clearly and in the least expected way. "Something" doesn't "happen" at all, but the Lord makes his presence known.

I tell in another place in this book about a student with a rare disease which had affected his foot and leg and about how we had had a service of foot washing that ended with our sense that he had accepted us as persons who shared his pain in the Lord.

That all started off in my mind as a story about how we accepted him, that is, the event itself had been powerful and moving. It was clear that we had all been present to each other in ways that we couldn't articulate. Yet the *event* had been clear, that is, it was an *Event.* The meaning of it was not so obvious. It became more obvious two years later while I was reading a book in a library. The book was not about anything connected with the particular events, though it was about sacramental theology. The story came into my mind and I realized at once that we had not so much been there accepting him as he had been there accepting us, letting us into his pain and also letting us into his courage, which became more real for him as he was able to share it. In that moment, the student, his pain and courage became a Word from God, a Word of his acceptance of me in my stumbling and blind attempts to minister in God's name. My ministry was "spiritualized" through the Spirit acting in and through that young man. I believe that I would not have heard the Word two years later unless I had set aside time for prayer, time to let the Lord speak, time to let the words of Scripture wash through my time, time to hear what God had to say.

And that was an example of the times that "nothing happened," that is, the time I would walk for an hour and not "get anything." I did not "get anything" for days until one day when I was not "praying" the Lord let me know that he had known me and been with us all that night at the foot washing.

But mostly we are unwilling to wait and be open at all times for the Lord. We set aside some time each day for him and if he doesn't use that time to the best of his ability then we are sorry, but the rest of the day is simply not available to him. God must fit into our prayer or else he's out of luck. It seems to me that we must be as open to the Word when we are not "praying" as we are when we enter into a time of concentrated listening and thinking. Perhaps we ought to be more open to the presence of the Spirit speaking through all the voices of imagination around us.

We come at prayer the way we come at so many of the things in our lives. As I sit to write I realize that I have got to "get" so many pages today — in just the same way at prayer we feel we ought to "get" something. "Get" — another Word from the Lord to add to our list of spiritual notches. Thus a person consulting a spiritual director feels, probably inevitably, that he must have a "something" to say, there must be some victory this week, some progress, our Gross National Prayer must show more and more examples of our wringing insight from God. God is not, I think it safe to say, a giant private enterprise system. So we must listen to him to find out how it is that we can come to do things his way, the way of purity of heart, of intent made pure by him, the self recognized in the context of the realities willed by God (see Thomas Merton, *Contemplative Prayer*, Chapter XI). It is there that we "find ourselves in God's truth," which is where our truth was all along. The truth of that encounter in the chapel in the washing of a student's foot had been there but was hidden. One afternoon after praying and getting "nothing," reading a book became the moment when God could reach out and speak to me and enable me to reach out — who knows — to you.

God reveals himself in his own way, eliciting from us his truth when we are ready to hear it. I am one of those persons so full of ideas and thoughts that it is hard for me to listen to hear the word of God; his moment comes, as God knows and now as I know, when my defenses are down, when I am not trying. It is also clear that I would never be able to listen, to recognize those occasions and the Word, unless I had prepared myself to hear by recollection or being open to God speaking to me in his way and in his time.

So it is necessary to prepare the ground, necessary to dig oneself over, get familiar with what is below the surface, the good wormy human humus that is us, and fertilize it with the usual thing we fertilize with, that is, to follow out the metaphor to its inevitable earthly conclusion, to spread around our used-up thoughts and feelings and dig them in to whom we are. We do that by dragging out our past and our future, our needs, our history, and our hopes, that which makes us up emotionally and spiritually. It was because I had been doing that throughout some long mornings of walking and quiet thinking that I was able to hear the Word directed to me two years ago in that student, not the Word directed to him, but the Word directed to me in the event of his being accepted and accepting me. It was possible only because there had been preparation and readiness to hear, intention.

I realized also how far I was from the life which God had been urging me to live, that life of freedom, courage and strength. It is heartbreaking to realize that we are so separated from God. The strange, dreadful, but ultimately consoling thing about prayer is that while it brings us into contact with God it also brings us into contact with how far we are from him. The judgment comes with the love; they seem always to be connected in our relationships. For me, refusal of love, not refusal *to* love is the particular sign of my alienation from God.

For years as a minister I had been the one who loved other people. I took care of them, listened to them, arranged help for them, helped them to sort out their problems, put my arm around them, comforted them, got them out of trouble, encouraged them not to get into more trouble than they could handle, testified for them in court, believed in them, hoped for them, went out after them at night. I had done all that, not because I *ought* to (though I did do it because a minister ought to) but also because I wanted to — I liked doing it. I liked to help them, liked to be with them, liked to give whatever I could, whatever I thought best. I did all those things because I had chosen to be a minister, had been chosen to be a minister.

But one thing I needed to know, that I know now is that the Lord was telling me that I had also chosen at sometime not to *be* loved, not to be vulnerable by not accepting the love that people were holding out to me. The times people allowed me to help them were signs of their love for me, their willingness to be helped. They let me help them, brought me into intimate parts of their life, into their fear and hopes and despairs and bloody sweats. When they did that they were letting me do my job, letting me do what I wanted to do, letting me do what I thought I ought to do. By allowing me to reach out to them they were reaching out to me, but you see, however much I knew that in theory, I did not *know* that. And that's a spiritual problem with not only individual implications, but also corporate and political implications.

It was one morning in bed, turning drowsily to say something to my wife, that my distance from God hit me. It came first of all in knowing that I had never allowed her to love me as much as she does, which is greatly. These two thoughts, distance from God, distance from my lover, hit me simultaneously. I have a friend who says of such moments in his life, "What a kick in the ass!" By that he means, I guess, that it is a revelation which is not exactly ego boosting, but in the sense that it is true it is an enormously freeing and joyful thing. So I confess to you that when I discovered that I had always chosen myself first, always chosen to *do* for people, to *do* for God that I had not ever accepted what they and God had done for me it was "a kick in the ass." Those movements of love, from God and from others are the same movement. My wife, who knows me rather well by now, found it typical that I could not keep my mind on the business at hand, but instead blurted out just what it was that had come into my mind. There is a sense that what I announced to her that morning is that I am a sinner, as if she didn't know. But in that joyful and consoling moment I found what it was that had kept me from the reality of God's love for so long, just how it was in my own peculiar way I had constructed a reality centered around the fact that I was the one who did things for God and for people, and politely ignored the Lord who had reached out to me in his people in so many ways through so many people and in and through the humanity which is the Body of Christ.

> . . . first of all our meditation should begin with the realization of our nothingness and helplessness in the presence of God. This need not be a mournful or discouraging experience. On the contrary, it can be deeply joyful since it brings us in direct contact with the source of joy and all life. (Thomas Merton, *Contemplative Prayer*, p. 70)

So it was that I came to pray and to find my own reality in the heart of God. In unusual times and places, I found out that I really didn't want the love of other people or God, because in some way I had been satisfied only to love myself, to choose *me* and what I could do by myself before all others, to choose myself in such a way that I was unable to feel or to see the love which other people had lavished on me.

Such blocks have psychological roots and yet, on a simple and most profound level, I unlocked a door within me which enabled me to turn around and see that the lonely room in which I had been living — thinking it was all there was — was really full all the time, full of familiar faces, the lovely people who had been so kind, loving, and forgiving to me through the years. And so I was and am grateful to them and to God who revealed his will in us. And his will not just to me in the great courses of history but inside the heart; inside the deep place where I am, he speaks to me things I could not bear to think, things that I would never speak to myself, would never hear unless somehow I put myself in a place where I could hear the voice which spoke to me from the silence. And even then, there was a voice which drew me to that place.

All those mornings of walking through Cambridge, listening, praying, trying to force God to make the connections I thought he ought to make, and then turning over one day in bed to know suddenly the desolation and the love.

I'm not exactly proud of all this. It doesn't make a pretty story. Sitting here, it is not an easy story to tell. Nor is it the full story, just in case you thought I was being completely open and honest. Everything is conditioned, there are privacies which even I must respect in myself, things that are between me and the silence. Nor is the story over; doors are open and lights on but there is no guarantee that they will stay open or on. There is always a potential energy shortage; I can turn lights off and close doors at least as easily as open them and turn them on.

We are, all of us, good at that, and I am at least as good at it as you, dear friend.

I think of all those people over the years and what they would say if they read this. The one thing I know — they will be as forgiving of this as they have been of other things through the years.

The very knowledge of the love in which we are borne itself brings more problems, the sense of it brings more responsibility. I know now that I am more in control than I was. After a year of prayer and conversation with a spiritual director, I am more careful and more thoughtful of what I say and do, more ready to listen and hear, more ready to wait through long periods of not hearing, letting myself get the refusal to hear out of me, because I can make myself ready to hear the life-giving Word. Above all,

I think I know now the mystery of love offered in Jesus through his people.

But beyond that, I try not to let old habits take over. I must be as ready to hear what other people are trying to say — that they are reaching out to me, not only out of their troubles and their need, but out of their strength and their ability to love. I will not fall back into old habits of not accepting the love which others give, of being unwilling to recognize my own need to be loved, my own need to be reached out to. But I will refuse it and I will fall back into that isolation. I must learn to walk over and over again, this time with feet grounded in the love sent by God to me through the people around me.

So that and a lot more is the result of learning to pray that day on Huron Avenue in Cambridge. God wants us, wanted me, and still wants me to make a choice of self; he wants us to choose our own self, our real self, our self responsive and alive to the gifts of other people, ourselves alive and responsive to the needs of others, and this involves choosing ourselves. He has chosen human beings, as he chose to reveal himself in Jesus Christ, and this choice is the deepest reality in the universe. We have been reached out to by God not because we are good, charming, or interesting but because he is God and he has decided to choose us. That truth was hard won by God in Christ. We are chosen to share his life which is in Jesus Christ and it is a life which reaches out to live a new life in the midst of the old life and which sees the world in the way in which God must see us, transformed by his love into the realization of all its potential. One of the things that we mean by "love" is seeing something as it might be if all faults were removed and all potentiality for good realized, as God sees us. So we see the people and the institutions of the world, re-formed to serve those whom they now oppress. This too is because God has chosen us, everything flows from that, particularly our politics and our economic morality.

"It is not enough to go out of the Land of Egypt, one must enter the Promised Land." (St. John Chrysostom, *de disciplina Claustrali*, 22 P.L. 202:1129) It is not enough to say that we have listened to the voice of God in our lives and come to know that we are known in our hearts, we must go on to vision and hope, and struggle to bring about the fullness of the promise in Jesus.

We need to share that passionate love with others, not only with the people immediately around us, those with whom we have some personal relationship, and the people for whom we are responsible all over the world, for the hungry, the oppressed, and the godforsaken, but the choice of us all in Jesus Christ is a promise to all those yet to be born, those to whom we are tied not only genetically and ecologically, but in the state of being chosen by God. We are for them in hope, in all their potential, and in all God's promise. We do that only by aiming to make the world in which they are born a place where their human potential can be fully realized.

Whatever else that means, it principally requires political action. Prayer is not prayer if the only results are nice thoughts or a collection of oughts. Prayer calls us out to action. Our salvation in prayer and in the hope it brings for each of us is invalidated if we do not understand that the Lord who speaks to us on the corner of Huron Avenue speaks to all the people of the earth, born and yet to be born, and calls us to his freedom and his future.

If he has chosen them, who are we to hang back from

their promise? For every theological act and insight which has personal import, we proclaim another theological act and insight which has political import and which is never separated from the community of persons. This is because the reality of the world is that we know God only in the faces and lives of our brothers and sisters, as once men and women knew the glory of God in the face of Jesus Christ.

It isn't enough to bring ourselves out of desolation and wandering and loneliness and slavery; it is equally necessary to find and proclaim the Good News which speaks to us of the time of restoration of the land of promise, fulfillment, and joy. We find it when we realize it has found us and speaks hope to us in the midst of the struggle,

It is not enough for you to be my servant,
to restore the tribes of Jacob and bring back the survivors of Israel;
I will make you the light of the nations
so that my salvation may reach to the ends of the earth.

It is my experience that the light still shines, the bush still burns, and that we are enabled to walk on the road to the future by the gift of feet because we are grounded in prayer.

John F. Smith, an Episcopalian priest, is chaplain at Boston University. From 1968 to 1974 he was the chairman of the Boston University United Ministry and during that same period he taught humanities. He has been active in civil rights and antiwar activities on and off campus. During the past academic year, he studied and wrote on an Underwood Fellowship in the area of prayer and spiritual life. He was a contributor to the book, *Community on Campus*, and has had numerous articles published in both secular and religious journals. He received his B.A. degree from the University of Michigan and his B.D. from Episcopal Theological School. He is married and has two children.